Understanding Small Period Houses

Understanding Small Period Houses

Amanda Laws

The Crowood Press

First published in 2003 by
The Crowood Press Ltd
Ramsbury, Marlborough
Wiltshire SN8 2HR

www.crowood.com

British Library Cataloguing-in-Publication Data
A catalogue record for this book is available from the British Library.

ISBN 1 86126 600 6

Acknowledgements
My thanks go to the numerous researchers and writers who have directly or indirectly contributed to this book, and to the owners of houses, many of whom have readily offered encouragement and ideas. Lastly, an acknowledgement of support must go to my family, and particularly to my father, who taught me from an early age to look beyond the shop fronts of Chichester to the Georgian architecture above.

Special thanks to English Heritage, The Landmark Trust, The National Trust and The Victoria and Albert Museum.

All drawings by Alan Werge-Hartley.
All photographs are by the author, unless otherwise credited.

Frontispiece: Rose Cottage, Upper Swanmore, Hampshire (Grade II)

Typeset by Carreg Limited, Ross-on-Wye, Herefordshire

Printed and bound in Singapore by Stamford Press Limited

CONTENTS

1. INTRODUCTION

Houses are defined either by the period in which they were originally built, or at the point at which they were substantially altered around an earlier house. The quality of the materials used, the design and its relation to other houses in the region also help to explain them. They become important historically when enough time has elapsed for them to be seen in the context of the period in which they were built, and, as in the study of history itself, several decades need to pass before a true perspective can be established. For most people, period houses need to be significantly different from the contemporary architecture around them, and the latest generally accepted definition of 'period' is that of the Edwardian era, or perhaps a little later if the classic detailing of the 1930s is included. However, some houses built in the middle of the twentieth century contain specific design features worthy of consideration, and these can now also be regarded as period houses.

This book is an introduction to the subject and a starting point for those wanting to know more about how houses have developed, whether they are owners of a period home or just interested in buildings. I have chosen to concentrate my efforts primarily on England, as Welsh houses are, in most cases, indistinguishable from those in Herefordshire and Shropshire to make an individual study necessary, while many northern English and Scottish houses deserve a book of their own.

A large part of this book is dedicated to unravelling the mysteries of why houses look the way they do, why and when certain materials were used, and how all buildings have been shaped by economic, social and artistic influences. There is a natural tendency to oversimplify and generalize in order to make sense of

centuries of development over a wide geographical area, but where this has occurred more detailed reading will correct any misunderstanding. Those interested in the development of various aspects of building and design will benefit from visits to museums, houses open to the public, and by reading more specific publications. In doing so, they will develop a greater understanding of domestic building. When we visit houses open to the public, the way the house was lived in and by whom is as fascinating as the design and its stylistic features. The history of our own houses, while often less detailed and colourful, is exciting to research, helping to explain how the original house looked and how it developed into the property in which you live today.

How earlier owners used the space around the house is equally fascinating, although in this area we are much more dependent on looking at the styles created for large-scale projects. Many small period houses would not have had gardens laid out around the property, and so designing a garden in keeping with your seventeenth-century house will be more about a sense of history than historical accuracy.

Examples I have used are mainly of small- and medium-sized houses dating from the sixteenth century to the early twentieth, though the book does refer to larger houses and encourages visits to those open to the public. Also included are houses that were built with little or no outside intervention, usually described as 'vernacular'. They were built of a local material in an empirical manner traditional to the region and have few or no conscious references to the 'polite' architecture of the time. In addition, there are other houses which were influenced by the look of local large properties and, after the eighteenth

Farnham, Surrey (Grade II) An eighteenth-century brick front added to an earlier timber-framed building, with the later use of metal wall ties to keep it attached. The garden ornament depicts a pine cone (not a pineapple as is often thought), which was a popular symbol representing fertility and wealth.

Bishopstone, Wiltshire (Grade II) Netton Old Farmhouse, built in 1637 of chequered flint and limestone, is an example of a simple vernacular house.

century, by the many publications that had become available. These were more modest versions of the fashionable houses of the time, but, like doll's houses, mimicked the details and proportions.

Grade II listed properties represent the largest category of historical buildings and many of the houses featured in this book are currently termed Grade II. Some Grade I listed houses are included as these are useful as historical guides,

and there are many unlisted houses that warrant inclusion.

The Restoration of Period Houses

Old houses are often a collection of styles and periods, as previous owners adapted and altered their homes to suit their changing needs. From the latter part of the twentieth century, protection for buildings of historical and architectural

Downton, Wiltshire (Grade I) The Moot is an excellent example of 'polite' architecture, circa 1700, built from Flemish bonded brick with a projecting central bay, a modillioned pediment and twelve-pane sash windows.

Melbourne, Derbyshire (Grade II) This early eighteenth-century two-storey house was substantially altered the following century when the roof height was raised to allow for an extra floor with dormer windows. A Victorian bay was added on the right-hand side (since removed) and the position of earlier attic windows can also be detected on the unsymmetrical façade. (© Kim Laws)

significance has halted this process, in order to preserve what still exists from further inappropriate alteration. This was an essential move in the case of many houses, but strict building regulations and some conservation officers with rigid ideas will naturally lead to much less innovation in adapting our living spaces than in previous centuries. Some people enthuse over the contrast of Tudor panelling juxtaposed with an eighteenth-century plaster ceiling, but, if legislation of the sort we live with now had been written earlier, such eclectic combinations may never have existed.

Most period homes are not true to a particular time or period. Although improvements made during 'treasured eras', such as the Georgian period, are celebrated, many of us have to learn to accept later alterations as having an equal value that will probably only be seen as such by future owners. The uncovering of important features, such as shutters, panelled doors and fireplaces, is often the process in which a period homeowner is engaged, but the removing of the later features is ethically debatable and sometimes illegal. As part of the process of preservation, there is a strong argument for allowing subtle and harmonious alter-

ations to continue in tandem with restoration, unless you own a 'time-warp' house (a house from one period with little or no alteration) and some enlightened conservation officers allow this. It is likely that these twenty-first-century improvements will be seen in 200 years as significant evidence of our changing needs, much as we now regard Georgian sashes installed in a Jacobean manor.

The real issues lie in the sympathetic development of a house, using appropriate methods, quality materials and craftsmanship and having a sound understanding of the house, its history and its place in the locality.

The Influence of Location and Events on Town Development

England's historic towns and villages have developed through the migration of the population to certain regional places with naturally occurring advantages, such as a river crossing. In many towns the early street arrangement was designed by the Romans, Saxons or Vikings. Those of Roman design are often based on a T- or cross-shaped plan of streets, and despite later alterations this layout can be seen in places such as

Thame, Oxfordshire (Grade II*) *Market stalls in the centre of Thame became permanent buildings and the early sixteenth-century Birdcage Inn is part of that redevelopment. (© Kim Laws)*

Chester, Chichester, Farnham and York. Early examples of irregular patterns of streets often followed natural changes in level or other features, such as fortifications. At St Albans in Hertfordshire the fortifications followed the position of earlier walls. Early encampments became established villages and, with possibilities for trading, grew and became towns.

Towns designed in the medieval period were usually based on a grid pattern and all had at least one main street. Where a town did not possess a market square, one street would be very wide to accommodate the market, such as at Marlborough in Wiltshire. Some of these streets have since been encroached upon, as

permanent shops replaced market stalls, leading to a reduced street width. Building plots in towns were long and narrow, with small street fronts as in Ledbury, Herefordshire, where they measured 18 × 200ft (5.5 × 60m). These were known as burgage plots, and were a means by which the landowner divided land for rent to tradesmen. As land became less available in towns, houses grew taller and plots were subdivided, creating buildings behind the street front and requiring narrow alleyways to connect the street to the rear properties. These alleyways have a variety of names depending on the county, ranging from 'twitterns' in Hampshire to 'ginnels' or 'wynds' in parts of Yorkshire and 'jitties' in the Midlands. Some of these later became the 'courts' so vilified during the late nineteenth-century slum clearing era.

Most towns and villages have seen swings in prosperity, linked to local trade; and a growth in trade could transform a village into a substantial town. The extent to which house building increased from the middle ages and in which areas, had a great deal to do with local economic initiatives, the health of the population and, in the sixteenth century, living in a more stable environment under the Tudors and the Stuarts.

A downturn in a town's prosperity resulting from something as simple as the silting up of an

Titchfield, Hampshire (Grade II) *These houses are evidence of a remodelling of earlier timber-framed village houses in the middle of the eighteenth century.*

Stamford, Lincolnshire (Grade II*)
Improvements to the River Welland in 1673 brought some prosperity to Stamford and as a result the houses on St Georges Square were remodelled.

estuary, as happened in the sixteenth century at Sandwich in Kent, produced what we now term 'time-capsule' towns. Where there was no money to update fashionably, the houses stayed close to their original vernacular style. This was often coupled with the natural decline in the population of a local community, made worse by outbreaks of plague, smallpox, typhus and influenza. Changes in land distribution resulted in the abandonment of some populated areas (2,000 lost settlements recorded).

In contrast, new villages and towns have appeared. Model villages were designed and built by landowners and philanthropic industrialists, while new towns were created as a result of improved transport networks and a middle-class desire for a town in the country. During these changes in the prosperity and suitability of an area, the houses within it altered. High-status houses were sometimes abandoned and pillaged for their building materials and hovels were upgraded and rebuilt to become important dwellings. The changes that have occurred in a house, whose footprint may have been apparent for half a millennium, is the most interesting study as it combines sociology, demographics, the history of public health and local economic development.

CASE STUDY:

Description

Rookery Farmhouse is a four-bay, lobby-entry house, probably originally of timber frame construction and modernized at various stages since the seventeenth century. The external walls are built of a mixture of local knapped flint laid in courses and English bonded brick, in what appears to be quite arbitrary sections. There is a central quatrefoil chimney stack that dates from the seventeenth century, as well as three later stacks built on external walls. The doorway is set into a Dutch gabled, double-height porch. A badly eroded datestone on the gable wall indicates family initials and a date of 1655 for the updating of the property, a date confirmed by the early metal casement window also in the gable wall. A numbered Royal Exchange Assurance firemark also attached to the porch gable is for the year 1795, but the records for this year no longer exist. A second

Location: West Sussex

Date: Updated in 1655 from an earlier house

Type: Lobby entry (Grade II)

updating took place sometime in the Georgian period, but this was much less ambitious and consisted mainly of the changing of windows from metal casement to wooden sashes. The interior shows detailing from the seventeenth and eighteenth centuries and includes fireplaces, panelled doors and plank-and-muntin

ROOKERY FARMHOUSE

panelling. Small windows in the roof space are evidence that the attic, with its own staircase, was used as living accommodation sometime in the past. As with most farmhouses, the messuage included a granary, general-purpose barns and a dovecote likely to date from between the seventeenth and eighteenth centuries.

History

The Scardevilles, originally from Normandy, arrived in this area of Sussex in the thirteenth century and there is evidence of the family residing in Funtington 200 years later. They may have farmed from the original timber-framed house, as the first John Scardeville and Miss Fortune were living there by the time their first son was born in March 1655, which coincides nicely with the major updating of the house. Their marriage is indicated on the datestone by the two initials F and S. They had five children, with their eldest son John taking over the house with his wife Dorcas. It is probable that the third John Scardeville with his wife Jane added the Georgian features at the time of their marriage circa 1730 and, despite infant deaths, they managed to bring up six children in the house, including another John. As his son, the fifth and last John Scardeville, and his brother Thomas had died without issue by 1855, their sister Elizabeth Sadler and her sons took over until around 1903, when, after at least five generations of the Scardeville family at Rookery Farmhouse, the property was finally sold. The legacy of this family can still be found around Sussex in an anglicized version of the name. Scardefield crept into use in the family in the eighteenth century and may have been due to misspelling the surname rather than an effort to disguise their French roots.

The design of the front windows was an attempt to modernize in the eighteenth century. However, due to the limiting height of the front wall the upstairs' sashes had to be inserted sideways, as can be seen by looking at the proportions of the panes. They are not Yorkshire sashes, which are designed to slide sideways.

The porch dates from the first period of improvement and has a rubbed brick four-centred arch leading to the front door. The door itself is six-panelled Georgian, now half-glazed.

On three sides of the house chimney stacks were added in one of the later periods of updating, partly hiding the remains of seventeenth-century attic windows with brick moulded dripstones.

A reclaimed gravestone found in the garden is engraved with the names of two of the great-grandchildren of the first Scardevilles. Both Elizabeth and Anne died in infancy in the 1740s and this badly eroded stone may also be in memory of William, who died a decade later.

2. HOUSE HISTORY

Researching the history of your house will give you two kinds of information. Firstly, it will go some way to explaining why your house looks the way it does and, secondly, you may discover a slice of social history that makes living in the house more enjoyable. You will see how your house relates to other buildings in your area, as well as to the wider picture of architectural history. Modest period houses have usually undergone considerable change, either in use, status or looks since their original construction, so keeping an open mind and seeing beyond your first impressions may reward you with some unusual historical findings. Understanding how your house developed will help you to become more sympathetic during any future restoration work and more informed in your use of methods and materials. What you find out may be of interest to local history groups, will always be of interest to future owners, and in some small way will undoubtedly be a contribution to the study of social history and domestic architecture.

Recognizing Styles

Before you start researching, it is useful to understand the development of houses, including materials and the methods used, both locally and nationally. This knowledge will put your house into context and help you to interpret the visual and documentary evidence that you find. For example, most owners of Victorian terraced houses will not see the link between the word 'hall', as in their long, thin room behind the front door, and the wide room of a medieval hall house, but that is the origin. Having general knowledge about styles of building, the use of materials and the social and economic issues that have shaped the property will help to explain its

Stamford, Lincolnshire The features of this early eighteenth-century building are lost behind an extension. Coved eaves, plaster swags and demon masks all point towards a once important façade.

important features and can be a start to dating the original build or a period of significant updating.

The designs of houses evolved from the traditional methods of the region, accessible materials and a keen eye on what prosperous local landowners were building. Many small houses up to the nineteenth century have evidence of architectural features that first appeared in the fashion-conscious country and town houses of

Dedham, Essex (Grade I) Originally part of the sixteenth century Queen Elizabeth's Free Grammar School, the facade of Well House was rebuilt in gault brick with red brick dressings in 1732 by the headmaster Thomas Grimwood, and was the school attended by the painter John Constable.

Shrewsbury, Shropshire (Grade II) The Crescent is divided into two building periods and the earlier houses are circa 1790. An estimate of the date can be achieved by looking at the fine fan-shaped overdoor light, the corresponding 'tympanum' above the window, the thin glazing bars on the sash windows (without horns) and the use of cast iron for the railings.

the wealthy. Starting in London, building styles appeared in various parts of the country at different times and house historians need to be aware of this 'architectural time lag' when dating details. In addition, the 'local builders' vernacular' (a distinctive regional variation or local interpretation of a recognized fashionable style) can confuse when dating from history books alone. For a long time, these builders' interpretations were based on word of mouth and the odd sketch, resulting in the range and sometimes quite eccentric collection of detailing and proportions on medium and small regional houses. It was not until builders' pattern books were published in the eighteenth century that less idiosyncratic interpretations were produced and a uniformity of house styles really began to evolve.

By the eighteenth century, especially in major towns, building was not controlled solely by the whim of a builder. Early in the century Acts of Parliament, taxes and local by-laws were all impacting on the style and detailing of house exteriors. Taxes, like those on windows and bricks, altered what was affordable, while some Acts restricted the use of combustible materials on the façade. If the seventeenth and eighteenth

Clare, Suffolk (Grade II) This fifteenth-century timber-framed house has undergone substantial alterations, firstly from a hall house to two storeys in the sixteenth century and secondly with a new Gothic front added in the early nineteenth century.*

centuries concentrated on building sound structures and preventing the spread of fire, the nineteenth century tackled health and sanitation. Acts of Parliament throughout this century provided the impetus to clear slums, provide council housing and create utopias for the middle classes, turning outlying villages into suburbs and devising garden cities to produce the best of both worlds.

Gathering Information – Contextual Evidence

The position in which your house stands in relation to other buildings helps to explain its history. Many towns and villages have grown naturally from the most important element of the

Moretonhampstead, Devon (Grade II) Pitt House, circa 1700, survived the village fire of 1845. It has a late eighteenth-century façade with Victorian sashes and window surrounds flush with the stonework, showing that no by-laws existed at this time to enforce the 1709 London Building Act.*

area, for example a crossroads, quayside, bridge, church or castle. The rest of the area will then have grown outwards from this centre, so in most cases older houses will be located near this founding element. Outside the original confines of a village or town, individual houses were built, then, with the later urban sprawl around a settlement, these older houses and even whole outlying villages were gradually subsumed into the main town. Many existing farmhouses were built during the Queen Anne and Georgian periods, when the Enclosure Acts imposed changes in land use. Farmers tended to build in the centre of their newly acquired lands and earlier farmhouses, perhaps not now recognized as such, tend to be found closer to the centre of populated areas. An early period house, now in the middle of a highly built-up area, may have once been a farmhouse, having been altered several times over 300 or 400 years.

Early street names can give a clue to the destination of the road or to the purpose of the buildings along it. Some origins are clear, for example Church Street and Bridge Street, while others indicate occupations, such as Butchers Lane, Weavers Lane and Fish Row. Others commemorate famous people, battles or other events, as in Waterloo Place and Jubilee Street,

whereas some require a little more investigation, such as Hythe Place (Hythe being a Saxon word for harbour), or where a street has been named after a local landowner. Knowledge of local history can help to identify street names that have changed from their original, as often happened when houses became 'gentrified' and the name was altered to be more in keeping with the new status of the residents. Castle Street in Titchfield, Hampshire (where there is no castle) has recently reverted to its original name of Frog Lane, aptly named as residents frequently trip over frogs in their gardens.

Original house names are equally fascinating and can sometimes pinpoint when a house was built to within a decade, for example names such as Trafalgar or Wellington. Other names relate to the builder or owner, or to a local dignitary or national literary figures like Byron or Wordsworth. Obvious house names are ones that relate to the look of the house, such as The Red House or Wisteria Cottage, or those linked to a past occupation, like The Old Post Office. There were fashions for where a house name should be located and many late Georgian and early Victorian houses have their names painted in the glass panel above the door. The generic terms used to describe a property can also be telling – the Victorian house builder was fond of ascribing 'Lodge' to a new property even though

Portsmouth, Hampshire (Grade II) Lombard Street, named after a group of merchant immigrants, wealthy enough in the seventeenth century to update this row of houses in the fashionable style.*

Lyme Regis, Dorset (Grade II) Library Cottage was originally two timber-framed cottages (and also once a library) and was updated by the architect Arnold Mitchell, adding two enormous eighteenth-century rainwater heads and a cistern reclaimed from elsewhere.

Bath, Somerset Gateposts were a useful place to attach the house name, and Elgin Villas were probably built during the Victorian period when the term villa was popular and when classical antiquities were being imported into the country.

it was not used as such. The name 'cottage', usually referring to a single-storey countryside hut, was often given to quite a substantial house to create a romantic vision. Likewise, the term 'villa' was attributed to great swathes of nineteenth-century superior middle-class dwellings to give a continental feel to the property.

House names were at their most popular during the Victorian period, but, as the postal system developed, the requirement to identify houses by number reduced the need for names. Bristol, for a long time the wealthiest and most forward-looking town after London, acquired house numbers as early as 1775. The original numbering of houses along a street was even numbers on the right and odd on the left, starting at the main road. However, changes may have occurred since the original plan, such as a road being renumbered, and this should be borne in mind when looking for a house by number in historical documentation.

The relationship your house has with the land around it and its neighbours will give clues to its social position in the area, any changes in status and possibly how long the plot has existed. In medieval towns the manorial burgage system of dividing land shaped towns and gave many houses their ground plan or 'footprint' and the garden length, even if the present house is significantly newer than the plot itself. Assessing the position of the house in relation to its neighbours and making a comparison either in whole or in the details can explain how your house came to be in its position. Some houses face a street while others are side on, which is often determined by the space available, the gradient of the land and the shape of the design. The older your house, the fewer examples you will find to make comparisons, so start by looking at your neighbours' houses, then the ones in the next street or in the next village or town, looking for similar features. The main structural material will help to date your house, as most areas only had one, or possibly two, main building materials until transport links made cheaper haulage possible in the nineteenth century. Whether your house is built of local material or an imported brick or stone will assist in the dating process, and changes in the structural material can indicate an addition or alteration. Often smaller period houses imitated larger properties close by in their use of materials and fashionable detailing, so also look at the most prestigious properties in your local area.

Gathering Information – Verbal and Visual Evidence

Discussions with neighbours, long-standing residents in the area and past owners are all helpful ways to build up a picture of the history of your house and its surroundings. As in any element of oral history there will be local 'hearsay' and fading memories, so it is important that, where possible, events and stories are supported by documentary evidence. This method may reveal the history of the past fifty years of your house and enable you to make the link to documents, such as the parish records and census returns. Often builders would be wise to consult locals before developing land to discover what may be hidden underneath. Lower Farringdon, near Alton, in Hampshire recently suffered with winter flooding and in particular a group of newly built houses was under water for some time. One elderly local recalled that the plot of land they had been built on had always been a pond when he was a child. So local knowledge can be invaluable.

Examining your house and making a detailed survey of your findings is another important way

Dedham, Essex (Grade I) Incised graffiti carved by eighteenth-century schoolboys into the soft red brick on the façade of Sherman's Hall, the English School founded in 1599.

Faversham, Kent (Grade II) This row of sixteenth-century houses has retained its jetty, but without the removal of plaster on the middle house, the origins of these houses would have not been so obvious. There is contrast of window shapes and glazing, from the original casements to Georgian sashes and Victorian bays. Divisions between the cream house and the blue one indicate that there is a substantial flying freehold between these two houses.

to understand its history. It is the roof and plan that should tell you clearly what type of house it is. Draw out a plan, marking the key positions of the fireplaces, external doors and staircase and any changes in floor levels which could indicate additions to the house. Draw or photograph details, both structural and decorative, indicating measurements, and list the visible materials used. Accurate measured plans can identify strange elements, for example flying freeholds in attached houses. This is where the dividing wall between the two properties is not strictly vertical, and the buildings overlap each other, giving one house part of the floor space of another. This may have originated from the landlord of the properties dividing the buildings to suit the

arrangement of his tenants. An extreme example exists in Odiham in Hampshire, where one house has, in addition, the first floor of the house next door, while the latter has the ground and top floor, accessed by the staircase that misses out the floor in the middle.

From looking at the drawn plan it may be possible to identify an original early shape of building that has been subsequently added to on various sides. In terraced houses built at the same time, the additions to an original building are usually restricted to the rear, although small additions to the front are possible. Some houses may have diminished in size due to a change of use or an accident, such as a bomb during the Second World War, and this change may be

Bosham, West Sussex (Grade II) *Development may be as obvious as this example, where the symmetrical façade with two side chimney stacks, built in 1743, has been altered by the addition of a single bay to the right, made apparent by the straight vertical mortar line in the brickwork and the change in fenestration.*

detectable by comparing early and later maps. If your house is on the site of an earlier house (which is quite likely if you live in a major town), there may be evidence of an earlier basement or cellar. Look for evidence of change, both in structure and in the use of parts of the house, as this could give you clues to its history. Scan the outside of the building for alterations to the structure, such as changes in material, roof pitch or window size.

The origins of a house are more likely to be discovered at the sides and rear of a property, where it was less important to update. With both stone and unrendered brick, straight vertical joints of mortar, or changes in the shape, colour or texture of the building material, often identify additions and alterations. Changes in brick can be very noticeable from the size, proportion,

bond and colour, while differences in weathering can reveal various ages of brick and stone. The type of mortar is not such a reliable indicator, as original lime mortar is soft, and, unfortunately, likely to have been replaced at some time with cement. Changes of material around a window may indicate a change in size or proportion of the aperture, or it could mean it might have once been a door.

Checking to see if the windows line up or match in size and proportion is a useful activity. Windows of two different opening types on the same building, for example casement and sash, often indicate a period of improvement. A change in window style was a fairly cheap method of updating a property, but sometimes only the façade of the house was altered, leaving the side and rear with the original windows. A

Salisbury, Wiltshire (Grade II) *Sash windows have been added into this seventeenth-century house in all but two apertures, with one breaking the line of the horizontal banding. One original mullioned window remains and another blocked-up version (out of shot). The Victorian door appears to have been inserted in another window aperture.*

house, the roof covering could have been renewed several times during the property's existence. Alterations also occur in the type of roof covering, such as a thatched roof being changed to tile or slate. It is the pitch of the roof that indicates what surface material was originally intended, although with some houses the pitch itself was altered by raising the walls, and a contrasting material added below the eaves can indicate this. During the eighteenth century the fashion was to hide the roof behind a parapet and so the roof shape of many houses cannot be accurately viewed by looking at the façade.

Inside the house, the changes that have occurred may be less obvious, unless you are prepared to remove recent decoration and plaster. A thick internal wall may indicate that it was once on the outside of the property and irregular walls can hide earlier structural timbers. If you are lucky enough to have a house that has not suffered the clean sweep of a developer, then peeling back existing wallpaper may reveal decades of wall covering, though this process needs expert advice to avoid losing precious information. Early wallpapers can also be found hidden behind architraves and skirting boards, so it is worth checking carefully behind fixed

Bridgwater, Somerset (Grade II) Built in the early eighteenth century, this house has obvious alterations. A shop window has been inserted on the ground floor and an external door has been blocked up (crudely with red brick); this may have been an external entrance to the cellars. Another window of a later date appears on the top floor of this side, set back a brick width from the surface, and there is a third colour of brick used in the alteration.

large ground-floor window may mean that the house was used as a shop in the past and census returns or trade directories can sometimes confirm this speculation. Blind windows are much more likely to be evidence of a change in the internal plan of the house or a designed feature to aid symmetry, than an example of window tax (*see* the example in Chapter Four).

Although it is unusual to find the wholesale replacement of the roof structure in a period

South Harting, West Sussex (Grade II) This late eighteenth-century house was two houses at one time. A ground-floor door is blocked up and there are differences in the window width between this house and its neighbour. The blind windows are part of the design to balance the façade.

Cerne Abbas, Dorset (Grade II) *The façade of this eighteenth-century house has some Georgian features, such as the use of expensive header bond and a blind window to balance the design, but the shape of the window apertures mean they could not easily be converted to sash windows and so are casements. Originally thatched, the iron roof and crudely altered shop window detract from the simple façade.*

Slindon, West Sussex (Grade II) *Well House has been extended sideways and to the rear, and was gentrified in 1694. This side view shows a distinct change in the pitch and the use of brick to raise the catslide roof.*

Clare, Suffolk (Grade II) *This seventeenth-century timber-framed house was wrapped 200 years later in white brick. The façade was given Gothic-style casement windows and was substantially raised to include a parapet hiding the old tile roof.*

items. The dating of period wallpapers can be achieved by a comparative study of existing examples, although accurate dating and conservation require a specialist (*see* Chapter Five). Clues can be found in the type and thickness of paper used; evidence of a tax stamp on the reverse will help to date more precisely, while motifs and colours are also indicators of age. Not many examples are found of early papers, due to paper being delicate and the fact that it is a likely interior detail to have been replaced.

Your house may have been subject to changes in the layout of rooms and the repositioning of doors and staircases, but, unless there is evidence on the outside or in ceiling joists or solid flooring, these changes are difficult to discover. In houses where the timber frame is exposed, the identifying of unused previously cut joints usually shows that a change in the interior space has occurred, often the removal of a wall to make two smaller rooms into one. Other timbers with illogical joint holes may be the result of timber reuse; in most cases, previously used timbers would be from an earlier house on the site or one close by. The reclamation of materials is apparent in the earliest surviving buildings, but the popular idea that many structures are the result of the reuse of ships' timbers is unlikely in the

Norwich, Norfolk (Grade II) A carved mullion window with an indication of the use of glass and originally on an external wall indicates a probable date of the early sixteenth century.

Titchfield, Hampshire (Grade II) This eighteenth-century wallpaper found in a loft space revealed an even earlier paper underneath.

Titchfield, Hampshire (Grade II) Timber floors can identify changes, as seen here where the blocks of parquet floor show the original position of the servants' staircase (now blocked up).

Broadhembury, Devon This simple cob cottage reveals a piece of carving on the staircase, unlikely to have been original to the structure, which may have come from the local manor house when it was updated in the early twentieth century. (By kind permission of the Drewe estate)

quantities claimed by owners, as this would equate to the wreckage from a sizeable armada. Dendrochronology, when it can be accurately used, can give a date for the felling of timbers, but will not determine the age of the present building, particularly if it is obvious that a reuse has occurred. Timbers that were new at the time the house was built need to be identified, such as the ones without additional joint holes, or the main structural timbers like wall plates, which are less likely to have been replaced during later improvements.

Recognizing fixtures and fittings that do not match the age or status of the property requires knowledge or thoughtful comparison from known datable items in other houses (*see* Chapter Five). There may be details in the house that are obviously not the same date as the structure, and many houses that appear on the surface to be of the Georgian period will have earlier structures underneath panelling and architraves. By contrast, Georgian detailing, such as shutters, may be hidden behind later attempts to modernize. Possible evidence of the reuse of fireplaces and other moveable items can add confusion, and the boom in architectural salvage in the last twenty years will make the future dating of some houses from architectural detailing alone very difficult.

The dating of your house from a datestone is also not as straightforward as it would seem. A datestone is a piece of stone, brick or wood with a date carved or painted on the surface and is often a structural part of the façade. Datestones, or marriage stones as they are called in some places, often mark a period of building activity, updating an existing house or improving it in time for a memorable event, such as a family wedding. Sometimes, later examples do identify the building of the original house and this sort of evidence clearly makes researching much easier. In some cases, other information is also given (the initials of the owners or builders are common), and occasionally the reason why the building was built. Insurance company firemarks can give some information about the history of the house and what was on the site at that date. House addresses are a relatively modern concept and up to the early nineteenth

a) *Moretonhampstead, Devon* Built by George Wills in memory of his wife.

b) *Slindon, West Sussex* This cottage of 1693 was substantially rebuilt in the Victorian period.

c) *Bisley, Gloucestershire* This datestone is on a chimney, dated 1682.

d) *Lavenham, Suffolk* One of a row of Victorian cottages, built by Thomas Turner in 1856, to house the workers of his wool-stapling and yarn-making factory.

e) *Faversham, Kent* An example of a pargetted datemark, marking a period of improvement for this sixteenth-century property.

Five datestones.

century the identification of a house was not straightforward. Where owners had insured their property in case of fire, a metal mark on the façade was required to ensure that the insurance company's brigade would attend and try to put out the fire. It was only at the introduction of the modern postal service in the nineteenth century that addresses began to be regularized so that firemarks became unnecessary, although some companies continued to issue them as a way of advertising. Original records are kept by some companies, while others are lodged at London's Guildhall Library. Although records are not complete, it is possible in many cases to identify the documents relating to a house easily if there is an identification number on the firemark.

Once all the available information about a house has been discovered, reference material is important at this stage to compare what you have seen. This takes the form of contemporary books on aspects of architecture, original architectural pattern books for both exterior and interior details, and builders' reference books for house plans. These can be found in museum collections, such as at The Victoria and Albert Museum and The Brooking Collection held at The University of Greenwich, London.

Gathering Information – Documentary Evidence

Researching the history of your house from documents can be a straightforward project if the dwelling was built in the nineteenth or twentieth centuries. The information available is more accessible and easier to read and understand and as there were a greater number of small homes built between 1800 and 1930, most researchers will complete the history of their house with relative ease. However, many owners with older properties will find the documentary trail going cold and will have to rely on the other comparative methods discussed earlier. Research can be a mixture of studying related material, such as the deeds, and looking at general books, for example the relevant volume in the Pevsner

Chichester, West Sussex
Firemarks can offer some information about a house, such as the number of rooms and what contents were inside. Numbered versions provide the most chance of matching the house with the details.

Architectural Guides: The Buildings Of England series. A combination of these research paths may yield the best results.

The first documents that need to be found are the deeds to the house. You may have been given copies when the house was purchased, but often these are only of the previous few years. Changes in Land Registry practice in 1925 made original deeds legally unnecessary, and the recent unforgivable practice by some institutional holders of documents of destroying papers has removed much of the evidence regarding changes in ownership and other financial transactions. All owners of period houses should request the original deeds from their solicitor on purchase or from their Building Society before more historical information is lost. Should you be lucky enough to have the original deeds for

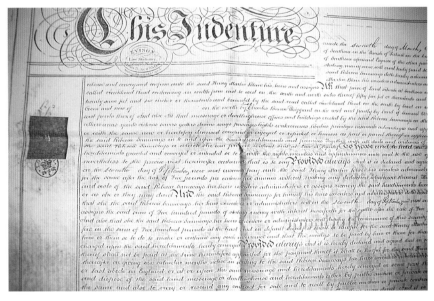

Deeds *Early documents, such as indentures, drawn up by solicitors are as difficult to understand as contemporary versions and have the added problem of copper-plate writing and worn paper.*

your house, then piecing together a clear picture of at least part of its history should be within your grasp (*see* Eaton Lodge Case Study in Chapter Five).

Studying early maps of the local area will reveal a quite different picture from today and will help to date your property or the properties around it. The first county maps appeared in the late sixteenth century, and these, with the addition of estate maps, enclosure award maps (both usually of the eighteenth century) and maps relating to tithes from 1838, all form the basis of this type of evidence. Early Ordnance Survey maps of the nineteenth century are clear and detailed and can be bought for easy reference, as can a large-scale contemporary map, centred on your house, to assist in your comparisons. Attempt to identify your house on various maps, starting in the twentieth century, and plot the position of the house in an attempt to discover what changes, if any, have occurred in the house

shape and surrounding land (*see* Railway Cottages Case Study in Chapter Four). Your house may at one time have been part of a larger estate and, if this is the case, information may be found if the estate papers have been lodged at the local record office. Studies by local amateur artists and photographers may have included your house at some time in the past and an early recording may show interesting changes to the exterior. Check the collections of the local library or museum, and it may also be worth contacting your local history society or photographic group.

Part of the interest in finding out the history of your house is to discover who the previous occupants were, which may be discovered through national and local documents, starting with the local library collection. National census information started in 1801 and was organized into towns, villages and streets. Examples from the early part of the nineteenth century are of

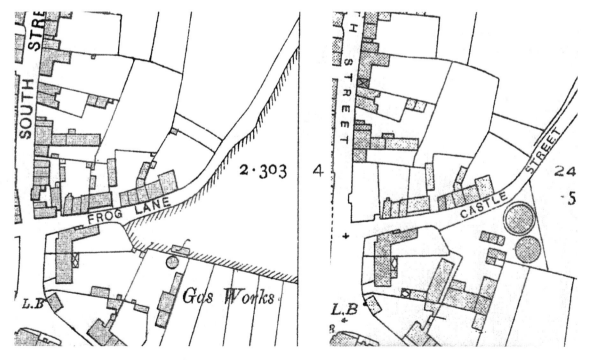

OS Map *Comparing OS maps of varying dates can reveal many changes. On the left, a map of 1909 shows a row of cottages on the corner of South Street and Frog Lane; on the right, by 1940 the cottages have gone and Frog Lane has been renamed Castle Street. (In 2002, it reverted to Frog Lane.)*

little use to the individual, as most houses are not identified individually and returns were not complete. However, they do serve to make comparisons regarding population numbers in particular areas across the century, as well as showing where around 6 million houses were built between 1801 and 1911. By 1841, the information is easier to interpret, and the later censuses, such as those of 1881, 1891 and 1901, are very useful indeed, but, depending on the format, you may need the owner's name rather than the address of the property. Nineteenth-century town directories, such as Kelly's Directory or White's Directory, are useful, particularly if your property was once used as business premises (a significant number of medium-sized houses were used as private schools); if not, it may be listed under the 'Private Residents' section. Wills and probate entries, tax returns and parish records are all informative and are usually located at the local record office. Check out their frequently excellent websites and guides to using these documents in order to understand the information and save time. The Internet is an invaluable source of information, as many amateur historians transcribe early documents for our benefit and the use of search engines can often find details of family names and addresses. Learning about the type of people who occupied your house gives a sense of its status at various times and therefore can lend weight to ideas on possible periods of updating. The accurate dating of the main structure of your house and its features will come from a combination of evidence

Titchfield, Hampshire *Records show that, in 1886, newlyweds John and Emily Fielder lived at this house; family history tells of the diamond in Emily's engagement ring being used to inscribe their given names on the window. When their family grew too large for this house they moved (see Mayburys Case Study).*

Titchfield, Hampshire (Grade II)
When this eighteenth-century lobby-entry house was refronted the following century, the keystones above the ground-floor windows were adorned with two faces. I would like to think these were the owners of the time, but without documentation this is whimsical speculation.

Sherbourne, Gloucestershire *The history of this nineteenth-century house, built using reclaimed Norman stone from a nearby church, should be possible to uncover because of its relatively late build and rural location that is unlikely to have been built on previously.*

gathered from all the sources discussed in this chapter, by making comparisons and by putting together a number of theories to be considered.

At this point, the use of professionals seems appropriate and there are many people, both local and national, who can assist you in interpreting your findings and extending your knowledge. Local building research groups, local history societies and genealogy groups may be happy to assist in your research. In addition, national groups relating to the age of your house, such as The Victorian Society, or museums specializing in architectural details, will be useful. It may be worth engaging a specialist in scientific dating processes or a material analysis expert, depending on what you have uncovered in the way of structure and materials within the house. Finding and studying documents is time-consuming, and, if you are unable to do this yourself, there are professional researchers who specialize in house history. With many period properties there is a massive amount of information to find and assess, and the information may often be contradictory and confusing. In addition, there are details to lead you astray, such as rogue datestones, and other architectural items reused out of necessity or in a mischievous attempt to deceive. The study of the interior may also lead to confusion when earlier details have been overlaid with later ones, leading to unsubstantiated assumptions based on particular features. Houses may not even be on their original site, or may have had substantial alterations that change their look entirely. For some owners, the history of their house and its past use is clear, but to many others the often conflicting evidence that they unearth is what makes the study of houses so intriguing.

Richmond, London *Reclamation can offer opportunities to confuse – this coach house was built, not in 1696 as the Latin inscription says, but in 1890, from a number of demolished buildings.*

Dartmouth, Devon (Grade II) *There is a natural assumption that houses were built in their present position, but this house was originally built at the bottom of the hill in 1629 as Dolphin House. Having suffered bomb damage, timbers were reused to create this smaller version.*

Leeds, West Yorkshire *Unfortunately, not a stained-glass window by the Arts and Crafts polymath William Morris, but made for the owner, Walter Mills, in 1939, incorporating his initials into the design. (© Alan Werge-Hartley)*

Yealmpton, Devon (Grade II) *Some houses have clear origins, like this early nineteenth-century Gothic-style tollhouse on the Modbury Trust Turnpike.*

Description

The southern section is the earliest part of this house which originally was a two bay lobby-entry timber-framed building with a service bay behind. The roof was hipped at both ends and there is evidence of a 'droke' (the Titchfield name for an alleyway) on both sides of the house, giving rise to reasonable speculation that the original dwelling was detached. The alleyways have now been subsumed into the house and have resulted in a flying freehold on one side. Around 1730 the southern part was updated with a brick façade of Flemish bond with burnt headers, the new style of fenestration and a parapet wall to hide the roof. At this point the size of the house was increased and the front door acquired a grand portico and was repositioned in the centre of the extended house. The next century saw a tall brick front added to the north section of the house, which

Location: Hampshire

Date: From 1550

Type: Lobby entry with Georgian additions (Grade II)

projected slightly further forward giving the appearance of two separate houses, as it is today. These puzzling façades have yet to be explained, but do offer an excellent opportunity to see the effect of the 1709 London Building Act. It took decades for local by-laws to follow London's lead in fire prevention and the time

MAYBURYS

lapse between the two developments is obvious, as the windows in the earlier house are flush with the brickwork (circa 1730) and the later ones are set back (circa 1800). In 1988 a front door was added to the north section to allow for the division of the property, by then too large for the needs of the average family. In the interior important features include plaster and wood mouldings, panelling and fireplaces and there is evidence from periods of updating in the eighteenth and nineteenth centuries.

History

In 1537 Thomas Wriothesley (later the Earl of Southampton) was given Titchfield Abbey and its lands and commissioned a survey to assess his estate, and this is the first evidence of a dwelling named Maybrayes on the High Street of this market town. The seventeenth century saw a general decline in prosperity of the area, but within 100 years there were signs of renewed growth in trade, confirmed by the rebuilding of houses like Mayburys. By the end of the century it was being used as a school for young boys called the 'Titchfield Academy', run by Mr R Dodd. This use continued for most of the next century, renamed 'Westholme', and the 1881 census showed that there were seventeen pupils attending the school with three teachers. By 1893 Westholme had reverted to a family house owned by the Fielders (a local brewing family), and at the turn of the century they returned it to its original name of Mayburys. There was a brief attempt to convert the house into a hotel in the late 1950s and it was finally divided into two dwellings in the 1980s when much of the gardens were sold off for development.

The façade shows two distinct building periods. The difference of height of the façades, the window styles and the position of the street front could never have created a unified appearance. The right-hand section, originally timber-framed, had a central front door and possibly looked like Pendean Farmhouse (see Chapter Four).

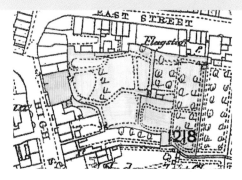

This Ordnance Survey map of 1881 shows the house with its façade and railings on the High Street. The garden shows paths, trees, outbuildings, a flagstaff and a row of lime trees near the house which survived until the 1980s.

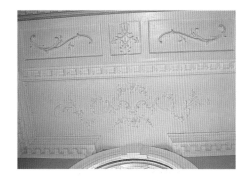

This plaster ceiling is unusual in a small provincial town property and is dated to the middle of the eighteenth century, when the house had its first development from a timber-framed structure to having Georgian detailing.

The house has a number of fireplaces, mostly from the Victorian era, apart from this Georgian replica of marble with a steel register grate added recently to a room where the chimney stack had been removed sometime in the 1950s.

Description

The original part of this house, most likely built during the summer of 1797, is timber-framed under a tiled and hipped roof. The wooden frame is horizontally flush boarded in oak and surrounds two symmetrical brick chimney-stacks. Other than the unusual construction for a Georgian house, the façade shows the classical symmetry of a pedimented doorcase and bay windows and the symmetry continues either side of the house with curved brick walls. Sometime after 1889 The Hut was extended to twice its size at the rear in brick of standard stretcher bond. Other than an eighteenth-century black and white Purbeck marble floor the interior is primarily made up of features from the Victorian period. These include simple heavy marble fireplaces and plasterwork in the form of corbels and cornices.

In 1964, due to massive deterioration of key

Location: Hampshire

Date: Summer 1797

Type: Timber-framed and clad (Grade II)

timbers such as the sole plate, the house required complete rebuilding, and what exists now is a replica of the original, other than the doorcase and central window. Building regulations at that time did not allow the house to be rebuilt using original methods and materials, so the front walls are now blockwork clad in

THE HUT

timber. However, if the house was being restored today, conservation officers would have ensured that its restoration was undertaken to the original specifications. Attached to the façade is a firemark from the Phoenix Company, though on investigation the identification number appears to be for another property entirely.

History

In September 1796 John King, well-known locally for his shipyard on Sweare Lane (now King Street), bought out his partner and prepared to build himself a new house alongside the yard.

Rather than build with brick, as so much of Emsworth was at that time, he used the shipwright's skills with timber and saved himself a fortune in brick tax. In about 1900 his granddaughter wrote that she had been told that the house was built in one long summer's day, and, if this was an accurate recollection, it would make the build date the summer of 1797. The speed of build would have been made possible by the shipwright's skills in prefabricating the timber frame and erecting it around the previously constructed chimneystack. Brick was used for the curved walls either side of the house which connect the house with the shipyard office, now a garage. Mr King was an elderly man and only lived a few years in his new house before it became the residence of his son John. By 1881 John had retired and his son William was running the shipyard and living at The Hut, while his sister ran a small private girls' school nearby. In 1891 William's widow was living in the house, but it was soon leased and finally sold in 1948. It is currently lived in by only the third family in its 200-year history.

The façade shows a symmetrical two-storey house with double-height splayed bay windows with glazing bars. The window joinery has horns, which would not have been part of the original windows. The central gable features an arched window and the doorcase complete with pediment and fanlight.

The eighteenth-century doorcase complete with metal fanlight under a pediment decorated with open dentils. The door itself is half-glazed and Victorian.

The open string staircase with its decorative stair ends, hand-turned balusters and mahogany handrail is indicative of the late eighteenth century and therefore likely to be the original, rather than a Victorian improvement.

The late Victorian addition to the house has been given plasterwork detailing in the form of corbels and cornices. The cornice in the main living room has a typical classical grapevine motif.

3. METHODS AND MATERIALS

The builders of early houses acquired an under-standing of their materials and developed ideas by seeing the way that other houses were being constructed locally. As no truly speculative builders existed until the seventeenth century, individuals erected houses for themselves and their family using local craftsmen with specialist skills within the village. Houses were built from available materials, the widest range of which can be found in towns close to a river, where the local material could be supplemented, expense permitting, by the importation of other materi-als. It is surprising how far inland small vessels could take cargoes and, with the Thames navi-gable up to Oxford, the Severn to Shrewsbury, the Trent into the Midlands and the Ouse to York, a great deal of the country had a choice of more than one building material. However, the dependence on local availability in some areas continued for many years until two important changes occurred. There was a re-emergence of the skill of brick making (lost since the Roman period) in eastern coastal regions as early as the fourteenth century, as one of a number of tech-niques brought over by immigrant workers from Europe. This meant that, in areas where clay was available, builders could construct with brick. This industry, when coupled with the development of effective transport systems in the form of canals in the eighteenth century and rail-ways in the middle of the nineteenth century, brought about significant visual changes to many towns and villages. At some point in the seventeenth or eighteenth century most populat-ed areas had a period of rebuilding, but there are a small number of 'time-capsule' towns where, at the point when new materials were easily available, the area lacked the prosperity to rebuild. As a consequence, the local material has

Dartmouth, Devon (Grade II*) This house, circa 1635, is likely to be based around an earlier house. It was built from stone on three sides and, other than the ground floor shop front, has retained its original timber-framed façade.

continued to dominate, creating a real sense of place.

Once a range of materials was available it became clear that a mixture of materials was the logical approach, allowing each to be used appropriately. From the early medieval period onwards, many fires had wiped out whole

Lewes, East Sussex (Grade II) Bartholomew House is an early nineteenth-century building covered in black glazed mathematical tiles. The two-door arrangement is mostly likely to represent a main door to access the entertaining rooms and a tradesman's door with steps down to the basement.

communities and it became obvious that timber-framed construction needed modification if it was to survive. The solution was to build fire-walls of stone or brick between buildings and sometimes this included the back wall. The latter became known as three-quarter houses, early examples of which can be seen at Dartmouth in Devon, where timber for the façade arrived by river and locally sourced stone was used for the rest of the structure.

By the sixteenth century, good house-building timber was becoming expensive so, as transportation methods improved, more structures were built of a combination of materials. This practice was employed for the updating of existing buildings or for finishing and detailing purposes. For example, where stone was not available, such as in Essex, brick became the main building material. In some cases, the choice of

Titchfield, Hampshire (Grade II) The brick façade in English bond of the seventeenth century hides a timber-framed Wealden house.

Weobley, Herefordshire (Grade II) Stawne, an early sixteenth-century sandstone and timber-framed house, with evidence of the owner's wealth seen in the use of close studding and carving.

material was as much aesthetic as practical, with expensive materials being used in an attempt by the householder to elevate his status. The wide distribution of building pattern books and the creation of local variations of London styles in the eighteenth century saw the beginning of the modification and finally the abandonment of truly vernacular houses.

Structural building methods fall neatly into two building types, frame and mass. Traditional 'frames' were built solely of timber, until the Industrial Revolution brought sufficient understanding of wrought and cast iron to produce the metal frame. The roof timbers were usually part of the main timber structure in early buildings and once erected a range of materials was used to fill in the gaps of the frame. Materials used for building in a 'mass' method include mud, stone and brick, but these still required a timber-framed roof structure.

Timber-Frame Structures

Timber-frame construction is the earliest form of prefabrication, and is more about carpentry than building. The method consists of a frame, which is braced and divided into sections by wall timbers of vertical studs and horizontal rails with an infill in each section. Early frames were often built straight on to the ground, although those that have survived are the ones raised on solid plinths to keep the timbers dry. Newly felled or

'green' timbers had their joints cut and marked, the timbers were assembled and held together with pegs, and the building was then 'reared' using many people. Scored 'carpenters marks' on structural timbers (designed to identify the interlocking parts) were made with different tools, depending on location and time period, and were often Roman numerals with other distinguishing marks. The green timbers were soft enough to work easily, but this meant that, as the timbers dried, houses warped and twisted, giving them the character that is so recognizable in early structures. Some timber buildings are measured in 'bays', which is the distance between two vertical posts and their corresponding roof trusses.

Weobley, Herefordshire (Grade II*) This building is a single-bay cruck-framed structure, although at this end the cruck blades have been replaced on the ground floor by brick.

Titchfield, Hampshire (Grade II) Easily identifiable carpenter's marks line up these two timbers on an internal wall of this fifteenth-century house.

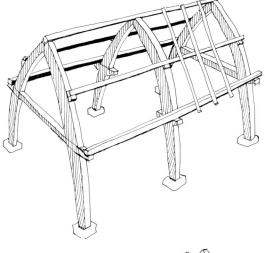

a) **Cruck** *In the cruck method, both the walls and roof are formed with pairs of curved timbers braced together. Material was often used to cover the timbers, completely concealing the frame and making it impossible to identify this method from the outside.*

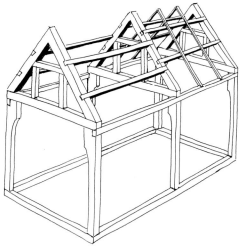

b) **Post and truss** *The post and truss roof is made up of vertical posts supporting a triangular frame or truss. The trusses, in this case Queen posts, are constructed at regular intervals along the length of the roof, with the common rafters attached to purlins to complete the frame. Like the cruck it forms both the walls and roof, but allows a greater internal space.*

c) **Box frame** *The box frame is separate from the roof and does not require the roof truss to support it, therefore the roof is only required to take the weight of the roof covering.*

   Both the box and the post and truss methods can be built with a number of variations of roof types, and both methods can be found across the country.

Types of timber frame.

Oak has always been the favoured building wood, as managed oak forests originally covered vast areas of the country. As the need for suitable timbers in these forests increased and prices rose, local timbers such as the poplar (found in cruck buildings in Herefordshire and Worcestershire) made acceptable alternatives. Each section of the tree had a specific use, and once the main timbers were cut and the secondary wall timbers fitted, the small offcuts were used for wattles or laths in the construction of the wall.

The treatment of exterior wall timbers and panels, both for weatherproofing and fashion, varied from county to county and included lime and tar. Initially, the panels between the timbers were filled with thin woven laths of wood called wattle, which were then enmeshed with a mixture of mud and clay known as daub. These panels were often covered with a lime render to weatherproof them, then painted in one of a variety of regional colours. The naturally found oxides produced yellows and reds; in some areas bullocks' blood was used to colour the plaster a deep pink. Although the blacking of timbers and the whitening of panels was not a widespread surface treatment and is mainly attributed to the Victorians, there is some evidence of it being of late eighteenth-century origin. Wattle and daub had a limited lifespan, so in many cases the panels were eventually replaced by brick nogging. The whole façade might then be replaced by brick as fashions changed.

There are regional and chronological variations in the timber-framing method, resulting, for example, in the different appearance of a timber-framed house found in Shropshire to one in the south of England, and of a fifteenth-century house to a seventeenth-century one. The increasing cost of timber from the late sixteenth century and a greater understanding of both method and material led to later builders producing lighter timber frames with the timbers

Lavenham, Suffolk (Grade I) This section of Shilling Old Grange has panels of wattle with a covering of daub (now possibly plaster).

Steyning, West Sussex A mixture of flint, stone and early brick in English bond with timber framing above and a later infilling of basketweave brickwork, all under a stone roof.

a) **Weobley, Herefordshire** *The Red Lion Inn was built of heavy, widely spaced timbers some time in the fifteenth century.*

b) **Lavenham, Suffolk** *This example, also built some time in the fifteenth century, shows close studding of slimmer timbers.*

c) **Singleton, Sussex** *Bayleaf Farmstead shows a more economical use of timber in this Wealden house of the fifteenth century.*

d) **Ledbury, Herefordshire** *Church House is early seventeenth century and is late to be using close studding.*

Regional and chronological differences in timber framing.

being further apart. However, the amount of timber used was also a demonstration of wealth, and so, while a building with a greater amount of timber should indicate an early example, this is not always the case. The status of a building can be deduced not only from the quality and quantity of the wood itself, but also from the carving that has been undertaken both inside and out. Houses like Rufford Old Hall (1530) in Lancashire show close studding and decorative timberwork, and at Little Moreton Hall (1450)

in Cheshire the rectangular panels are so totally filled with decorative quatrefoils of wood that it is impossible to distinguish them from the frame.

The jetty, or overhang, on a timber-framed structure was a development of the box-frame method and identifies an ancient building to most people. This practice started in both urban and rural areas at the time when upper floors were introduced into hall houses, peaking during the sixteenth century. The reason for projecting the upper storey outwards on timber-framed

Shrewsbury, Shropshire Timber framing with decorative 'quatrefoil' additions to the panels.

buildings is the subject of much speculation. It may have been a constructional solution to adding a floor without disturbing the existing house frame. Certainly it was a way to ensure that your neighbours knew you had an upper floor, while also having the benefits of protecting the lower walls and increasing space. Jetties were also built at the sides and back of buildings, both in towns and rural areas where there was no land restriction, so it would appear that the taste for the contemporary architecture is an alternative reason for new houses being built in this manner. Prestigious buildings had elaborate carving and this, in conjunction with continuous jetties in towns where ownership of street fronts was expensive, showed wealth. Early jettied houses had just a slight overhang, but this increased later from a few inches to over 2 feet (60cm), requiring extra support in the form of brackets and offering even more timbers to decorate. Wealden houses are a regional variation of the jetty and are found mainly in the south-east of England, although a handful of examples have been found elsewhere. They appear to be a transitional stage between the open hall house and one with two usable floors, as they consist of a central open hall with two-storey jettied sections at either end. An example can be found at the

Weobley, Herefordshire (Grade II) This house of post and truss construction was once jettied at both the front and rear. The rear jetty has now been filled in with stone as part of an outshut under a catslide roof.

Coggeshall, Essex (Grade I) This house was built circa 1500 by John Paycocke, for his son Thomas, a cloth merchant, and shows close studding at its best. A continuous jetty along the street front with carved vine-leaf decoration leaves no doubt as to the status of Mr Paycocke. The position of the front door has been changed from being alongside the carriage entrance, an alteration that may have occurred in 1910 along with changes to the windows.

Bignor, West Sussex (Grade II*) A fifteenth-century, three-bay Wealden house with a large roof overhang to throw off rainwater, and flint and brick infill in between the timbers, where originally it would have been wattle and daub.

Rye, East Sussex (Grade II) The façades on this row of fifteenth-century houses show changes in the surface covering. Some show their structure, but others have been weatherproofed. Changes in window design are also apparent, firstly from casement to sash and then with the addition of Victorian bays tucked under the jetty.

Weald & Downland Open Air Museum, West Sussex, and many exist in altered form around the south.

In the seventeenth and eighteenth centuries, when fashions changed, many houses that were originally jettied had the lower floor built out to meet the upper floor. This underbuild is often impossible to detect from the outside. Other houses merely had the timbers covered over with plaster, with the jetty shape still evident.

After the sixteenth century the price of oak increased for house building, as much good-quality timber went to the shipbuilding industry, and as a result this was the period that saw an increase in the reclaiming of timbers from earlier houses. In some cases, where the better homes were being rebuilt in brick and stone, timbers were reused in more modest dwellings, sometimes giving a humble cottage the carved timbers of a more prestigious house. The evidence of reuse is often the cause of much ill-informed speculation. The reclamation of timbers from dismantled ships (for example the timbers from USS *Chesapeake* being used to build a watermill in 1820), while not unheard of, is highly unlikely to the extent suggested, and is certainly illogical in parts of the country far away from the coast. One suggestion is that the phrase 'ships' timbers', having been passed down in local folklore relating to a particular house, actually refers to the wood or copse where timbers were intended for shipbuilding. Perhaps the timbers were substandard and therefore offered to local builders as timbers that had been grown, but not used, for ships.

There are two periods in history when timbers were visible on the outside of houses. The first was, of course, the medieval period through to the Tudors, just before wood became scarce and brick popular. The second was the Victorian period when the fashion for the 'Tudoresque' appeared and some buildings are so authentic that they could be mistaken at first glance to be of the earlier age. There are also bizarre examples, such as at The Red Lion in Southampton, where a genuine fifteenth-century open hall has been faced with Victorian fake timber. In-between these two periods the timber frame was covered in one of a number of ways, although in some areas this was always the local building style.

Roof Structures

The spanning of a roof space has been a continual problem over the ages, with many different solutions having been found. Stone arches,

Titchfield, Hampshire (Grade II) The rear of this timber-framed house has a typical catslide roof extending the living space. The house has been extended further in the Georgian period by a separate building grafted on to the catslide, which, when seen from the side, creates an M-shaped roof. The right-hand section of this house, originally timber frame, was covered in the seventeenth century by brick complete with pilasters.

domes and vaulting were all devised to bridge a wide, open interior, with only an occasional post or column for support, and are familiar sights in churches and cathedrals. Domestic buildings developed more modest roof structures and the design of the house was largely controlled by the possible roof span. When there was a need for extra space it was often produced by an outshut covered by a catslide roof, or, as in the case of an M-shaped roof, by effectively creating a second parallel building behind the original. In many aspects of building, local methods came from problem-solving initiatives by local builders. A combination of timbers to support and brace was devised and modified, and it is interesting that there were such similar good structural engineering solutions produced across the country (although perhaps the poor solutions simply fell down). Wood types used for roof construction were primarily the same as for the timber frame. In both walls and roofs the size and weight of the timbers reduced as an understanding of stresses improved and timber costs increased.

Roofs are made up of a timber frame with a surface covering, which creates one of a number of roof shapes. The roof frame is called a 'truss' and roof types are normally named after this main structural component, for example the crown post truss. As these structures are not visible from outside, it is unlikely that a full picture of the regional pockets of each type has been accurately recorded. Although medieval king posts have been found primarily in the northwest of England, examples of all types of roof structure are still being discovered, with a much wider distribution in the eighteenth and nineteenth centuries.

There are three main types of roof truss in period houses, the King post, the Queen post and the Crown post, with regional variations in methods of bracing, and it is this roof structure and its pitch that often give the most clues to the age and development of a building. The pitch of a roof is rarely altered and therefore the steep pitch required for thatch is often retained when the covering is altered to another material. For centuries a particular roof covering would have been dominant in a certain area, but, unlike the main structure, this would have been replaced during the existence of the house and changes made as other materials became available. Initially, trial and error must have proved that each roof-covering material worked best at a particular angle or pitch. The smaller the unit used, the greater the pitch needed to avoid leaks,

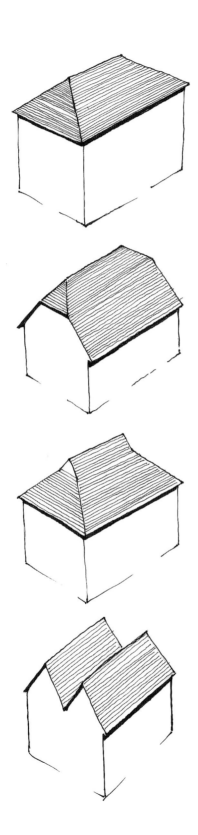

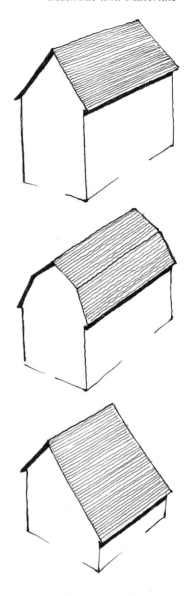

a) Hipped.	b) Gabled.
c) Half-hipped.	d) Gambrel.
e) Gablet.	f) Catslide.
g) M-shaped.	

Roof shapes.

Broadhembury, Devon The angle of the pitch and the raised stone gable ends indicate an original roof covering of thatch, as is still the case on the ridge.

so a pitch of 50 degrees was common for thatch, 45 degrees for tiles and 35 degrees for stone, with large slates being as shallow as 25 degrees. Lead or zinc could be almost no pitch at all as they were laid in sheets.

As with all other building materials, availability and fashion often dictated choice. A typical Georgian town house required a shallow pitch so that the roof could be hidden successfully behind a parapet and therefore tile or stone were used. A lightweight thatch of sedge, reeds, heather, grass or straw was the most common roofing material for cob houses. Although many previously thatched buildings were resurfaced with slate or tiles in the eighteenth and

Cley next the Sea, Norfolk (Grade II) Sunbeams, built 1710–20 of locally found pebbles, gentrified and extended with a brick façade, Dutch gable and a nineteenth-century porch. Traditional black glazed pantiles cover the roof.

Stamford, Lincolnshire (Grade II*) *These two houses have early eighteenth-century façades onto St Georges Square and show two standard roof shapes. The left-hand house is hipped with two rows of hipped dormers and the right-hand house has gabled ends with gabled dormers. Thinner glazing bars on the main windows of the right-hand house indicate a slightly later build date, whereas the bars on the windows on the left-hand house (other than the Victorian ground-floor sashes) are thicker.*

nineteenth centuries, cob houses tend to remain thatched. With the mechanization of farming, machines started to produce straw that was too short for thatching, and so alternatives were sought that were longer-lasting and less of a fire risk. Shingles or wooden tiles, usually of oak, were also an early roof covering, used as late as the eighteenth century, but these were inflammable and expensive. So slates and clay tiles became the main roof covering in many areas from the seventeenth century, with their fire-resistant qualities leading to a reduction in the height required for chimneys. Slate was a light-weight roofing material, shipped by sea from Wales to many coastal and riverside areas, but inland it was still expensive to deliver until the canal and railway systems were in place. Glazed roof tiles are most commonly found in East Anglia, where the Dutch influence in building was prevalent.

Roof shapes divide generally into two forms, the hipped roof and the gabled roof. Both of these shapes have many variations and there are imports from abroad like the Mansard, from seventeenth-century France, known in England as the gambrel. The ends of gabled roofs require protection from the elements and bargeboards were added for this purpose. Often elaborately carved and pierced, the earliest examples are medieval and, as one would expect, many

a) **Ludlow, Shopshire (Grade I)** *The Feathers Inn, which is sixteenth century with later additions, shows the use of bargeboards and other timber detailing so often copied by Victorian architects.*

b) A Victorian example, also in Ludlow dated 1874, with pierced bargeboards, an ornate pendant and quatrefoil carving on the panels.

Bargeboards.

Victorian versions also exist. Since the seventeenth century only a few changes have occurred in the construction of domestic roofs, and there is a legacy from early techniques of roof building still evident in modern methods. The development of the steam saw in the eighteenth century speeded up the process of cutting and allowed standard pre-cut beams and posts to be made, while more precise calculations of stress enabled the size of timbers to be reduced. Parts of Georgian roofs had no pitch and were made of lead, but complete flat roofs only became fashionable during the 1920s and 1930s. While this was a successful method in most Mediterranean countries, early flat roofs proved inadequate in most cases against the British weather.

Structures Built from Stone

Stone has been a readily available building material for a great many people for as long as we have built structures in which to shelter. But shaping stone was difficult, tools were crude and the small domestic buildings that resulted were very simple, unless skilled masons were employed. It is a building material mainly associated with grand buildings such as churches, of which early examples are abundant. However, there are some smaller early medieval stone houses in existence, such as Moyse's Hall in Bury St Edmunds, Suffolk (1180), and due to the durability of the material these early examples survive when few of their timber counterparts do. Stone was a popular material in the Tudor period, with small quarries being established anywhere there was suitable stone to find. The interest in stone during this time was an attempt to bridge the gap being left by the increasing scarcity and the rising cost of timber in areas where timber framing was the common method. It was also encouraged by the chance to reuse quality stone from demolished monasteries and to utilize the cheap labour of stonemasons made redundant by the Reformation. It continued its popularity into the 'Great Rebuilding' period leading up to the Civil War. The Parliamentary Enclosure Acts of the seventeenth and early eighteenth centuries redistributed land, which also encouraged new building.

Before canals and railways brought cheaper haulage, stone was only used for the smaller house where it was easily available. This placed the stone house into the landscape, the colour of the locally quarried stone matching well with its surroundings. There are still some towns and villages where little has changed in the use of building material since the eighteenth century. Places such as Stamford in Lincolnshire and Bradford-on-Avon, Somerset, are both good examples of a vernacular tradition of building surviving several centuries of modernization and change. Stone is widespread and varied, found in swathes across Britain and into Wales, with most types being suitable for building. The variety of stone ranges in colour, surface texture and durability,

Bibury, Gloucestershire (Grade II) Arlington Row was a fourteenth-century wool store before being converted into five cottages for mill workers in the seventeenth century. Built and roofed in Cotswold stone, houses like these were the inspiration for the later Arts and Crafts Movement.

with some stone being easy to carve and others hard enough to make detailed decoration impossible. Stone falls into two main categories, large units that have to be quarried, which include limestone, sandstone and granite, and small units found on the surface, such as cobbles and flint. The way that stone is secured together is similar to that of brick and although some dry walling took place for farm buildings, stones for houses were mortared together with clay or lime.

In some instances, to increase the strength and weather resistance of the lime or to use it sparingly, stone flakes called gallets were pressed into the mortar.

Limestones can be found from Dorset to Yorkshire and range from creamy white to grey. It is soft when first quarried but hardens over time, so most types can be carved and dressed. Somerset, Gloucestershire, Dorset and Oxfordshire all have limestones that are easy to

a) Derbyshire sandstone.	b) Bath ashlared limestone.	c) Yorkshire tooled gritstone.
d) Norfolk sandstone ('gingerbread' carstone).	e) Wiltshire flint and limestone.	f) West Sussex flint and French Caen stone.
g) West Sussex flint and stone with galleting.	h) Buckinghamshire square knapped flint.	i) Norfolk flint pebbles.

Types of stone.

Calverley, West Yorkshire (Grade I) *Calverley Old Hall has developed over a period of 300 years, starting in the fifteenth century and largely built of dressed and tooled stone. (© James Morris; reproduced by kind permission of The Landmark Trust)*

carve; Bath and Portland are well known and have been transported across the country at various times for prestigious buildings. Northern limestones, such as ragstone, are harder to work and are grey in colour. Chalk is a very soft limestone which generally makes a poor building material, however there are pockets of hard chalk through the Chilterns and towards Kent, known as clunch. A hard French limestone from Caen has been imported since the medieval period, and there are buildings constructed with it along the Sussex coast.

Sandstones give an even greater choice of colour and texture, ranging from pale yellow to dark red, and the effect of weathering also differs with each type. Sandstone from the north Midlands is an excellent building material in a variety of colours. Further north, gritstones, named because of their coarse texture, are

durable but difficult to carve, as with Millstone Grit, found around the Pennines. One of the hardest sandstones is called carstone, or gingerbread stone as it is brown in colour due to heavy deposits of iron oxide. Stone buildings are often rendered with lime plaster, making the stone difficult to recognize. This can be a way to protect poor sandstones or a cheaper option than the cost of dressing hard stone. Granite is the hardest of all stone and is found in Devon and Cornwall and parts of Cumbria and the Midlands, where it is also sometimes referred to as moorstone, when it is found on the surface as an outcrop rather than quarried. Houses of granite tend to be small and lacking detail, although a later example such as Castle Drogo in Devon is definitely neither of these things. Slate, although better known for roofing, can also be used as a solid building material, and

Snelston, Derbyshire (Grade II) *A seventeenth-century farmhouse built from red sandstone, made up of a three-bay house and a two-bay barn, so it may have originated as a laithe house.*

Luccombe, Devon (Grade II) *A seventeenth-century thatched cottage built of rough stone and rendered, which could easily be confused with cob houses of the area.*

Modbury, Devon
(Grade II*) Most houses in Modbury have their roughly hewn stone covered in a layer of plaster, but this early eighteenth-century house shows its randomly coursed stone (probably recently exposed).

Moretonhampstead, Devon (Grade I) *Built in 1637, these granite almshouses show some attempt at fashioning the hard stone on the façade, but at the side it is left rough. Blocks have been expertly cut, columns carved to produce the arcade and a flower motif and datestone complete the design.*

Drewsteignton, Devon (Grade I) *Castle Drogo, completed in 1930, is an excellent example of what can be achieved with granite when twentieth-century tools are available and money is no object. (By kind permission of The National Trust)*

Lyme Regis, Dorset (Grade II) *The well-known Arts and Crafts architect Arnold Mitchell built 'Sundial', a five-storey seaside home for his retirement, in 1903. It is built from local rubble limestone called blue lias, with contrasting stone dressings.*

evidence of the use of slatestone can be found in parts of Cumbria and Lancashire.

Once workable stone has been quarried it can be made into a regular block known as ashlar and its surface chiselled for a smooth or rusticated appearance. These blocks are used around doors and windows and often at the corners of the building, where they are called quoins. More expensive properties may have the whole façade built of dressed stone. These blocks, laid in courses, require very little mortar, while the best ashlar appears to have no joints at all. The cost of ashlar usually prohibited its use on small houses, and, as brick became affordable, the use of brick dressings was a cheaper option which also offered a contrast in texture and colour to a stone wall.

In coastal areas locally acquired materials were flint pebbles and cobbles. In some places licences were issued during the seventeenth and eighteenth centuries to those collecting building material from beaches; in Hornsea, on the east coast of Yorkshire, collecting was banned in 1869 to halt erosion. With a 'small unit' like flint, the method of building required immense skill to achieve precise corners, and so there is a history of constructing circular buildings when using small stones. After the sixteenth century, dressed stone or brick was often used for the corners and edges of flint and cobble buildings, with the mixture of materials producing highly decorative houses. Flints or cherts can be used directly as a building material, either collected or quarried, but are much improved by knapping. This is a method of breaking irregular stones to produce a good front surface, then working on them further to create uniform sizes with which to build. The edges can then be refined to make a knapped squared flint, a method that was employed more and more after the late sixteenth century. The discarded pieces of flint were also put to good use by being pushed into the soft lime mortar between the flints as galleting.

From the eighteenth century onwards, brick became the common building material for cheaper housing. Consequently, the fashion for brick waned amongst the upper and aspiring classes and stone saw a brief revival for larger houses. In the following century, with innovation in the form of machinery to cut and carve, stone also became widely available at a reasonable cost and this, coupled with increased large-scale brick production, was the end of the distinct regional appearance of towns and villages.

Structures Built from Earth

At the beginning of the twenty-first century, about one-third of all people in the world live in homes made from an earth-based material. Its

West Dean, West Sussex *This nineteenth-century flint and thatched circular building is an apple store in the picturesque style, complete with Gothic arched leaded light windows. (By kind permission of West Dean Estate)*

Lewes, East Sussex (Grade II*) Knapped flint in squared fashion with brick dressings and quoins on this eighteenth-century façade of an earlier house. Absence of glazing bars on the ground floor spoils the otherwise elegant façade.

Chichester, West Sussex Pebbles left unknapped, while charming, do not offer the proper level of sophistication on this provincial Victorian town house.

	b) *Sussex, West Dean The floor of the pergola with knapped flint and horses' teeth.*
a) *Suffolk, Eye Flemish bond brickwork of red and grey with inlaid shapes in pebble.*	c) *Norfolk, Cley next the Sea, Whalebone Cottage, circa 1760, made from flint, cobbles, stone, horses' teeth and sheep's bones.*

Three mixtures of materials.

use in Britain dates back to at least as far as the Romans and very likely a long way before that, with evidence of mud construction almost everywhere in Britain at some time in the past and continuing in some regions today. Generally, the method survived longest in parts of the country where brick, stone and timber were not easily available and were therefore expensive, such as East Anglia and the West Country, or in discrete areas where landowners chose not to update the houses under their care.

The ingredients for the earth-based method varied from place to place according to what was available, but started with the mixing of local earth with one or a number of other materials (straw, pebbles, lime or heather) and adding water. The more workable mixtures usually have a large proportion of clay in the subsoil and

Hayes Barton, Devon (Grade II*) *This house, circa 1450, is the very large cob house and family home of Sir Walter Raleigh, to which wings were added to give the house an E plan, possibly in honour of the Queen.*

often included dung in the mix. This may initially have been the natural result of using cattle to tread the straw into the mud, but early builders would quickly have seen how the dung increased the workable nature of the material.

There are three basic ways of building with this material in its unfired state and many subtle regional variations.

1. Starting with a plinth of stone and building rough layers or 'lifts' of the mixed material one on top of the other, allowing each to dry sufficiently to take weight of the next layer.
2. Building wooden shuttering on the site of the required wall and compressing the mixed material into the gap.
3. Using moulds to create unfired bricks, drying these as one would a clay brick and using a slurry of the mixture as the mortar.

Walls were thickly built, especially in the methods using a wet mixture. The two most important elements were the solid and water-resistant plinth, keeping the base away from the wet earth, and a large overhanging roof to keep the rain from touching the walls. The traditional advice is to give the building a 'stout hat and strong pair of boots', which, while particularly pertinent to cob houses, is a sensible idea for all building construction.

There are many regional names for this method of building depending on the county or country where it is used. Many of us would recognize the term 'cob', or perhaps 'adobe' used in South America and Mexico, but Welsh 'clom' or French 'Pise de Terre', meaning 'rammed earth', are less well known. Norfolk builders use 'clay lump', while in Haddenham in Buckinghamshire they call their local earth-building method

Broadhembury, Devon *This wonderful estate village is full of thatched cob cottages, with some having medieval origins. It has been carefully preserved by the local landlords, the Drewe family (of Castle Drogo), who bought much of the village property in the 1900s.*

'Witchert', but the methods and ingredients are similar. There have been local changes in the methods of making cob in various parts of the country in order to keep up with architectural fashions. Early in the nineteenth century some Devon builders changed to the wooden shuttering method in order to produce a greater degree of symmetry and smoothness for smarter-looking town houses.

Structures Built from Brick

In England, brick and tile making were common during the Roman occupation, but became a forgotten skill soon after, although the recycling of this early material is evident in most parts of the country. The importing of European examples started as early as the fourteenth century.

Not only were bricks and tiles imported from the continent, but in addition expertise in the form of skilled immigrants, especially from Holland and Germany. The techniques of rubbing and moulding soft red brick to create decoration came from Holland, as did the 'Dutch Gable', both of which can be seen at Kew Palace built in 1631. The first bricks from the continent are said to have arrived as ballast on barges engaged in wool export, but it is likely that they became a regular import cargo soon after. In the fifteenth century brick was mainly used to build castles, such as Tattershall Castle (1434), and palaces, but was beginning to be necessary for chimney stacks in smaller houses. The use of brick to construct small houses was very rare before the sixteenth century, although tiles were made and used earlier as roofing material, as

Sandwich, Kent The influx of immigrant brick-makers can be seen clearly in the small bricks in the side wall of this house, with the later standard bricks added below making a good comparison.

they were easier to produce and therefore cheaper. By early in the seventeenth century brick and tile were becoming common building materials for small houses, primarily in areas where clay was readily available and transport costs negligible.

Traditionally, autumn was the season for digging clay, as this allowed the winter weather to break down the material and improve its workability. In spring, the bricks were made, dried and fired ready for use in the summer months. Early bricks were often made from clay dug on the building site itself and fired in kilns or 'clamps' as they were called, fuelled by rough timber and subsequently by coal. Later, they were more likely to have been made in a local brickyard, of which there were many by the eighteenth century. Evidence of where local clay was dug and made into bricks can still be seen in many towns and villages, if only by the old street names, for example Brick Kiln Lane and Brickfield Lane.

Farnham, Surrey (Grade II*) An early brick row of almshouses, for eight of the town's poor (1619), is embellished with a crow-stepped gable above the entrance to a communal garden and has small bricks laid in English bond.

The size of the bricks produced was largely determined by the maker and they were probably modified by the size of the maker's hands, as bricks had to be picked up in one hand to be laid. Early bricks tend to be smaller, especially in areas where a continental influence prevailed, and they may also have been generally thinner to speed up the drying and firing processes. The 'Statute Brick' was established by The Worshipful Company of Tylers and Bricklayers in 1571 as 9 by $4^{1}/_{2}$ by $2^{1}/_{4}$ inches, and, other than a few increases in size during the Brick Tax period, bricks have only altered marginally since the sixteenth century.

Before the seventeenth century the construction of walls for the average house was left to the builder, with the result that the bond was usually quite random. Early walls were very thick, but over a period of time craftsmen realized that the bond type was more important than thickness to the strength of a wall. Various ways to strengthen walls were devised, including the use of buttresses, tie plates and, in the case of thin garden walls, of deliberately building a curving wall in a serpentine shape. In the sixteenth century English bond was the standard for important houses and by the seventeenth century, when the strength of certain patterns became universally apparent, economical derivations of English bond were more commonly used.

In the early days of brick making, making and firing methods were constantly being improved and early attempts often produced irregular brick shapes needing thick mortar or clay to even out the courses. Where mortar could be afforded, a mix of lime and sand was the most commonly used bonding agent on buildings before the nineteenth century, when cement started to be added to speed up the setting process. In early brick making, the lack of control of temperature and atmosphere during production led to warping, cracking and overfiring, the latter being caused by the relative proximity of the bricks to the flame. As methods were improved makers learnt to harness some of these variations for decorative purposes, particularly using the bricks darkened by the kiln flames to form patterns. Polychromatic brickwork became popular early in the sixteenth century for prestigious buildings, using burnt headers to create a diamond pattern called diaper work, of which St John's College, Cambridge (1511), is one of the best examples.

In the middle of the sixteenth century there was a dramatic increase in building when landowners acquired monastic land and

West Dean, West Sussex
This Crinkle-Crankle wall, circa 1810, is in the kitchen garden, its undulating, slightly angled build providing protected sections of the wall for fruit trees. (By kind permission of West Dean Estate)

a) Random bond.	*b) English bond.*
c) Flemish bond.	*d) Rat trap bond.*
e) Header bond.	*f) Diaper work in English bond.*
g) Chequerwork.	*h) Stretcher bond.*

Eight types of bond.

property, and to rebuild or convert these houses they made use of the increasing number of itinerant brick makers. By the end of the century, techniques in moulded and rubbed brickwork had been mastered, creating chimney stacks and dressings for the wealthier clients in a period that was later termed the 'First Great Age of English Brickwork'. Brick had become the primary building material in Hampshire, Berkshire and the areas in and around London, but it took longer to spread to the West and the Midlands, which were still well stocked with timber and stone.

It was not until the seventeenth century, as timber started to become scarce and therefore expensive, that interest in brick became more widespread. Events, such as the Great Fire of London in 1666, fuelled the enthusiasm for the material, and with a sudden need for housing it also gave rise to the 'speculative' builder. After the Great Fire, new legislation made it illegal in the City of London to rebuild in timber. It was also the catalyst for a number of other changes in house building and town planning, but these changes were not always adopted outside London. The practice of high-density building of timber-framed houses in towns and cities had led to earlier outbreaks of fire in London, Winchester, Canterbury and Chester, but it was the later fires of the seventeenth and eighteenth century that more obviously shaped the towns they had previously engulfed. In 1731 thatched roofs and a strong wind encouraged a fire in Blandford Forum to destroy much of the town and all but three houses in a neighbouring village. Blandford's subsequent rebuild in brick, during the following thirty to fifty years, makes it an excellent example of Georgian town

Aldbourne, Wiltshire (Grade II) In the building of this late eighteenth-century house, brick was used only for the façade and locally quarried stone was used for areas of less importance.

architecture. The demand for brick increased dramatically as its fire-resistant qualities were appreciated, methods improved and architectural influences flowed from abroad. In addition, the changes in the distribution and ownership of common land through the Enclosure Acts of the seventeenth century also gave rise to an increase in building.

By the end of the seventeenth century brick had become the major material in Britain for new buildings and for updating existing ones. Owners of timber-framed houses had a number of possibilities when it came to refashioning, if completely rebuilding in brick was too costly. The cheapest option was to remove the wattle and daub in between the wooden timbers on the façade and to replace it with brick nogging. However, the true age of the house would still be apparent and to hide the structure altogether one method was to attach tiles or imitation bricks to the timbers. These are called mathematical tiles and were a cheaper option than rebuilding the whole façade in brick, and in fact may have been the only solution where it was impossible to encroach on the pavement. A real brick façade, which was the most expensive option, required the removal of the structural timbers across the front of the building and their replacement with a brick wall. Although this was radical, in some cases it did allow the owner to create substantial changes to the interior by altering the ceiling heights and window proportions (*see* Rookery Farmhouse Case Study in Chapter One).

During Queen Anne's reign, a bond described as 'Flemish' became popular, along with a number of regional variations. It is associated with both Queen Anne and Georgian architecture, and it encouraged the use of burnt headers to create the chequer pattern that can be seen in almost any southern and eastern town. Flemish bond was extravagant in its use of bricks and so was often only used for façades, with a cheaper bond, or a different material entirely, employed for the sides and rear elevation. By this time, bricks were being made in a mould and by the end of the eighteenth century an indentation called a 'frog' had been introduced, impressed

into one side, to reduce the amount of clay used, and to assist in the drying of the brick and in its bonding when laid. Generally, the quality of brick making improved during the eighteenth century, with greater knowledge of making and firing techniques.

In addition to the effects during the firing process, it was the local clay that determined the colour of the fired brick, for example clay with high deposits of chalk produced a pale version called Gault brick, which was popular during the 1750s for above-average houses. Brick makers also learnt that by introducing other ingredients into the clay or on to the surface, the colour of the finished brick could be altered and the choice of colours increased. However, at the lower economic end of house building there was

Emsworth, Hampshire (Grade II) This pair of early nineteenth-century semi-detached villas are built of pale Gault brick on the front and red brick elsewhere.

no need for such a choice, as a high demand for properties encouraged shoddy craftsmanship from an increasing and uncontrolled workforce. Some builders produced thin walls of poor-quality clay and mortar, adding horizontal timbers in the walls as an aid to lateral strength. This practice weakened walls, already badly built, and such methods led finally to The London Building Act of 1774 being drawn up in an attempt to regulate the growing industry. Rendering the façade became popular during the Georgian and Regency period, becoming known as stucco, which had a number of benefits, including that of hiding poor brickwork, aiding weather resis-

Reading, Berkshire *Victorian Reading is known for its silver-grey brick, as can be seen on this house of the 1870s in Flemish bond with dressings in Staffordshire blues and red and white stock bricks as decoration above the windows.*

tance and producing a fair imitation of the more prestigious ashlar or fashioned stone.

In addition to building acts, in 1784 a brick tax was imposed, but, with a rapidly growing population and no viable alternative, brick building continued to increase and the number of bricks produced almost doubled between 1821 and 1840. At the beginning, the tax was calculated by number, so, to combat the tax, average brick sizes increased by up to an inch in depth. However, the 'Great Brick' from parts of Kent and Sussex had always been made and was the local traditional size until the tax doubled in 1803 on bricks over a certain volume. Tiles were also taxed and at a higher rate than brick, until Parliament repealed the tax on tiles in 1833 and on bricks in 1850. Around this time, early methods of making bricks in moulds were replaced by industrial processes, clay being extruded and wire-cut. This allowed the enormous quantity of bricks required for building the railways to be produced, which in turn enabled bricks to be easily transported around the country, thus removing the remaining regional variations in brick making that still existed. Victorian builders brought a new meaning to the word 'polychromatic brickwork'. For the first time, the average house could be patterned and colourful, and this, coupled with the Victorian enthusiasm for a multitude of styles and influences, brought about another great age of English brickwork.

Surface Coverings

The covering of a timber structure in wood, tile or plaster is an indigenous tradition in some areas and was primarily used to keep the weather from affecting the façade. Later, when only softwood was available for building and there became a greater need to protect the frame, the practice became widespread. Weatherboarding is a method of attaching horizontal planks to the façade, either flush or overlapping, and is seen in many eastern counties. The wood is painted a regional surface colour, which includes black tar in Essex and Hertfordshire, white in Kent and

Portsmouth, Hampshire *This villa (1905–10) is covered in white glazed bricks and is part of 'Brass Button Alley', the nickname for these houses which were mainly occupied by Navy officers.*

Cranbrook, Kent Wide horizontal close boarding
covering a timber-framed house.

Somerset, Devon and Cornwall slate hanging
has been a traditional method of covering the
structure, and there are examples of a variety of
shapes cut from the slate.

As the interest in new brick houses increased
and timber-framed houses became unfashion-
able, covering the surface with brick-shaped tiles
became popular in particular areas of the country. Mathematical tiling required unusually
shaped tiles that could butt up against each
other with a precision that gave the appearance
of brick. These were then attached to the façade
by battens or mortared into place, depending on
the existing surface. These tiles started to appear

*Cranbrook, Kent (Grade II) The original timber
structure is hidden on this sixteenth-century cottage,
which was built on a brick plinth with a part
weatherboarded and part tile-hung façade, with a
small pentice overhang.*

East Sussex and pinks and reds in East Anglia.
Sometimes the whole house is boarded or just
the façade and it can also be mixed with other
surface coverings. It is unlikely to be a coinci-
dence that in areas where weatherboarding is
common shipbuilding was an important local
trade. Flush and overlapping house-building
techniques mirror the shipbuilding methods of
clinker and carvel, and even surface treatments
such as black tar are in a boatyard tradition (*see*
The Hut Case Study in Chapter Two).

In Kent and Sussex tile hanging is a regional
method; like weatherboarding, it can be found
fixed to part or the whole of the house. The tiles
are attached in an overlapping technique, similar
to the roofing method, and have developed from
a vernacular tradition. In coastal areas of

Cranbrook, Kent (Grade II*) *The later alterations of Hill House hide a fifteenth-century cloth hall. During the eighteenth century the house was updated with decorative tile hanging, sash windows and a grand front entrance with Corinthian pilasters supporting a segmental pediment.*

Dunster, Somerset (Grade II*) This fifteenth-century row of cottages was built of sandstone and timber and was later slate-hung.

in the south-east in the seventeenth century, but became really fashionable at the end of the eighteenth century, when new houses began to be designed using this method. Examples mimic a wide range of brick colours. The use of mathematical tiles extends from Wiltshire to Norfolk, but they are found in the greatest numbers in the south in towns such as Lewes in Sussex. Often the reason for the increase in this method of refacing is attributed to the avoidance of the brick tax. However, there is evidence that, rather than being exempt, as tiles they were in fact

Lyme Regis, Dorset (Grade II) Originally three cottages, circa 1840, with a covering of hexagonally cut slates. It has retained its trellised iron porch and veranda.

initially taxed higher. They were also labour-intensive to make but, compared to a new brick façade, they were still a cheaper method of updating.

In many cases, covering the timber structure was also undertaken for fireproofing reasons. Although many towns destroyed by fire were rebuilt in stone or brick, after a fire in 1608 the timber buildings in Bury St Edmunds, Suffolk were rebuilt in wood, but this was lime-rendered to protect against future fires. Covering a timber-framed building with a lime-based plaster was initially confined to the panels in between the timbers, but as good timber grew scarce and smaller softwood frames were erected, plaster eventually covered the entire façade. The colour of lime-plastered walls varied in different locations, with early colours being the product of

Faversham, Kent Mathematical tiles are often difficult to distinguish from brick, but on this building the sight of weatherboarding to the side indicates a timber-framed building with a façade clad in tiles.

South Harting, West Sussex (Grade II) The edges of a building clad in mathematical tiles are often the giveaway, where the overlapping tiles are abutting the brick side-wall.

locally found oxides or other substances mixed into the plaster.

Pargetting, a medieval term for plastering which is now associated entirely with decorative work, is a regional method found mainly in Essex and Suffolk consisting of patterns and figurative designs. This sixteenth-century practice is divided into presswork (impressing shapes into wet plaster), high relief (freehand sculpting) and the use of moulds, with a tradition of the mould being left at the house for future repairs. The popularity in this form of exterior decoration was at its height firstly in the seventeenth

century, with a resurgence during the Arts and Crafts Movement and again more recently.

External lime-based plastering can be found across the country, not only covering timber, but also many other structural materials. In areas where hard stone was employed for building, such as in parts of Devon, plaster was used to smooth out the surface, which removed the need for the expensive use of stonemasons. Plaster has been used to cover brick and has sometimes been carved with indented lines to imitate ashlar, an early example being Oxnead Hall in Norfolk (1570). A fine plaster introduced from Italy in the eighteenth century called stucco, made with the addition of ground marble, was first used on interior ceilings in grand houses. But the term stucco is now used to identify any exterior render of the Georgian and Regency periods and is more likely to contain Portland cement, a Roman invention rediscovered early in the nineteenth century. Stucco became popular during the massive building programmes of the late Georgian, Regency and early Victorian periods. Early examples, if painted, were a dark, dirty yellow, but the better-known eighteenth-century stone colours are a variety of creams and greys. Some stucco houses were even painted in a trompe l'œil style, picking out the grooves of the imitation ashlar in a slightly darker tone to enhance the three-dimensional effect.

Later, it was necessity rather than fashion that required the covering of brick, as speculative building during the late eighteenth and early nineteenth century had unleashed poor building practices. Badly made or underfired bricks led to a need to protect and hide the surface, and as brick houses were less prestigious than stone at that time, rendering brick was the obvious solution. The use of strong colour during the Regency period saw greater licence taken with façades and influences turned from classical to the exotic, giving stucco an importance of its own. By 1900 stucco had ceased to be fashionable, with the 'truth to materials' doctrine ruling that the structural material should be celebrated, not hidden.

Weobley, Herefordshire (Grade II) This late seventeenth-century, timber-framed house was substantially altered in the middle of the nineteenth century, like its neighbours, and the façade stuccoed to hide the timbers.

Clare, Suffolk (Grade I) The Ancient House, a medieval timber-framed house of hall and cross-wing plan is pargetted in floral patterns and has a date of 1473.

CASE STUDY:

Description

Herefordshire is at the heart of the timber-frame tradition and villages such as Weobley, Pembridge and Dilwyn all have excellent early examples of timber building methods that have survived centuries of fashionable updating.

Luntley Court at Dilwyn is a five-bay, timber-framed house with a tiled roof built on a coursed plinth of rubblestone. The main part of the house and the cross wings are likely to have been built in the early seventeenth century, but most of this original external work is now hidden behind later alteration. The house was enlarged considerably, adding the grand two-storey porch with decorative bargeboards and dated 1674. The front door is battened and nail-studded with strap hinges in a fleur-de-lis shape. The interior has chamfered beams, early ceiling plasterwork and a staircase contemporary with the rebuilding period.

Location: Herefordshire

Date: Seventeenth century

Type: Five-bay, timber-framed farmhouse (Grade II*)

Within the curtilage of the house are several late seventeenth-century outbuildings, which seem to have been built around the time of the updating of the house. One of the barns close to the house appears to have been built using a section of the original house, as it has a gable with detailing unlikely in an agricultural

LUNTLEY COURT

building, such as dentil work and moulded door frames.

A pigeon house was also added during this time, as the law determining who could keep a pigeon house changed in the seventeenth century and yeoman farmers copied the lords of the manors in erecting their own live pantry. During the eighteenth century, with developments in livestock management, there was no great need to keep pigeons to eat and many pigeon cotes remained purely for their picturesque qualities. Its construction and detailing echoes that of the original parts of the main house with dentilled bargeboards.

History

The Luntley Estates were named after a gentleman of Herefordshire, John Luntley, who was alive around 1433. By 1540 Edward Bowyer owned Luntley and it was then bought by James Tomkyns, who was recorded as owner on his death in 1561 when it passed to his second son John. Clearly there could have been an earlier farmhouse on this site, although the original parts of the existing structure only date from the seventeenth century. Which of the next owners, the Capel family, the Whitmores or the Ferrer family, instigated the rebuilding in 1674 is unclear, however the Ferrer family were resident in Dilwyn at that time. Thomas Ferrer certainly owned Luntley by 1774 and his daughter, the last female Ferrer, married Tobias Davies and their granddaughter married Thomas Burlton. The Burlton family farmed at Luntley throughout the nineteenth century (335 acres recorded in the census of 1881) and the last direct descendant, Edward Myles Ferrer Burlton, sold Luntley shortly before he died in 2001.

The five bays can be seen in this image, four with gables and the fifth bay has been interrupted by a Victorian canted bay window under a small hipped tiled roof.

The only exposed part of the earlier house is the left-hand gabled bay, built of square panels with ornamental (concave quadrant) braces.

The main addition to the new house of 1674 is the double-height open porchway forming the third of the five bays. The porch has turned balusters on the open section and is decorated with carved timbers, moulded brackets and turned pendants on the corner posts.

In the field opposite the main property there is a timber-framed pigeon-house with a date of 1673 carved into the door lintel. It is rectangular in plan (as was common in Herefordshire), and the timber framing is similar to that of the house.

The early seventeenth-century dog-leg staircase has panelled risers, moulded strings and splat balusters (cut rather than turned), and carved ends to the newel posts, with pendant tops. The ceiling above has moulded plaster detailing of the same period.

Description

Baigens is timber framed with a later brick façade under a half-hipped tiled roof with a gablet and to the rear has a large catslide roof. The original front wall timbers that were once exposed are still evident inside the house and this close studding indicates a wealthy first owner. The house originally consisted of an open hall with a central fire or a smoke bay (early form of chimney) and unheated service rooms either side with a cross passage. Some time in the sixteenth century a central chimney-stack was built (later removed above the roof), chimney-stacks at the ends of the house were added (by the Hearth Tax Assessment of 1665 four hearths are recorded) and later an extension for a kitchen in the form of an out-shut built of a variation of English bonded brick. These improvements allowed the two unheated bays to be more comfortable and the

Location: Hampshire

Date: Late fifteenth century

Type: Four-bay hall house with cross passage (Grade II)

kitchen to become part of the house (before this time it would have been housed in a separate building as a fire precaution). Since the building of the chimney-stack there was no longer a need for the hall to be double height to allow smoke to escape and so an upper floor was added and to complete the improve-

BAIGENS

ments the walls of the main hall were given lavish wall paintings.

The house was divided into two around the middle of the eighteenth century and one dwelling refaced in brick, with the other following suit a century later. Other than this, the house escaped more radical remodelling in the Victorian period. The interior retains some historical detailing including chamfered ceiling beams and wide elm boards in the two principal rooms and evidence of the position of a high bench, common in medieval hall houses.

History

The earliest known information relating to this house refers to a man called John Bonvile and it is likely that he built the basic hall house sometime during the middle to late 1400s. By 1524 it was being leased to the Knight family, who were wealthy local clothiers, and it was probably John Knight the younger who had the wall paintings produced. His son Henry inherited the lease in 1559 but, due to financial difficulties, seems to have sold it to William Symondes of Winchester, and the property was named Symonds Farm during this time. (William was the brother of Peter, whose will of 1586 provided local education in the form of Peter Symonds' School in Winchester.) By 1606 the will of William Symonds left the house to be leased to Thomas Morey and Jane Symonds as a marriage settlement, with the estate revenue to be used to benefit Winchester's poor. By the middle of the eighteenth century the lease belonged to John Baigen and by 1769 the house had been divided into two, remaining in the Baigen family until the middle of the nineteenth century. The house was finally returned to one property under the lease in 1881 of James Pritchard, a music teacher, who finally bought the house in 1933. His daughters Hilda and Dorothy lived at Baigens until 1967.

The façade shows four main bays with a later outshut on the left built in English bond. Contemporary metal casement windows with wooden mullions and the door with gothic doorhead are in the style of the seventeenth century.

The façade appears to have been clad in brick in two distinct periods, a mixture of eighteenth-century random and Flemish Garden bond to the left and straight Flemish with blue headers to the right from the next century.

Small Tudor bricks indicate the early addition of this hearth. The bond appears to be English in some parts and random in others, showing that builders of the time were less knowledgeable concerning the relative strengths of bonds.

The original hall was updated in the middle of the sixteenth century with a moulded brick hearth with wooden bressumer, and wall paintings showing representations of hunting scenes. Zigzag patterns and flowers cover the timber verticals of the original façade, painted to resemble a textile wall hanging.

4. HOUSE DESIGN

During the medieval period house design developed slowly, influenced regionally rather than nationally by changing ideas, the availability of materials and the status and wealth of the individual house owner. By the seventeenth century, theories on domestic architecture were becoming known around the country, with both the well-travelled landed gentry and immigrant craftsmen offering new methods and ideas to local artisans. New architectural designs spread from London out into those towns and villages that were prosperous enough to rebuild in a more fashionable style and the proliferation of publications and pattern books in the next century provided the blueprint for change. House types were no longer regional and with a perceived need for 'off-the-peg' houses, speculators took the task of building houses away from owners to produce first grand Georgian terraces and then streets of modest Victorian and Edwardian dwellings. Other than a small proportion of innovative and well-designed examples, the 1920s and 1930s were swamped with borrowed architectural styles and hybrids, with suburbia growing from major cities as house owners moved towards a different lifestyle.

The Vernacular House

Although many period houses have been altered and extended over time, it is useful to look at basic house plans and some of the typical arrangements of space within small houses at particular times and to see the influence of early plans on twentieth-century homes. Initially, a dwelling was a single-storey room of varying size, but, over a period of time as living requirements changed, this space was subdivided both vertically and horizontally. The original building gradually altered and extended, often in a

Portchester, Hampshire (Grade II) Initially a symmetrical eighteenth-century house of three bays with lateral chimney stacks, wings at each end were added later, as were the Victorian bay windows.

random way, as owners added rooms and service areas when and where they were needed. These improvements frequently related to a change in the status and wealth of residents and, although in many cases it led to significant updating of a house, it could also lead to its abandonment as a principal dwelling.

A basic rectangular house could be extended in a number of ways by attaching extra bays to the sides. But if the house was in a heavily built-up area and plot widths had already been allocated, extending sideways along the street frontage would have been expensive, so it was more likely that a house would be given extra floors or a rear extension. At the back of a two-storey house the pitch of the roof could easily be continued, producing a single-storey outshut (under a catslide roof) (*see* Chapter Three). In addition, by flattening and extending the rear pitch, the internal space could be further increased, making use of the long medieval town plot. Only in rural areas could a change in the dimensions of the house be unconstrained; a

Coggeshall, Essex (Grade II) Houchins Farmhouse, circa 1590, is a timber-framed, double jettied, lobby-entry building. It is a brilliant example of local vernacular meets new fashionable ideas.*

Shere, Surrey (Grade II) *Possibly a hall of the sixteenth century and cross wing of the seventeenth, with a new chimney stack added on to the end wall. The timber framing shows evidence of both arched and straight bracing to the frame, while the panels on the cross wing have unusually been filled in with flint.*

projecting wing was often built adjacent to the original building, which produced an L- or T-shaped plan. These were called hall and cross-wing houses, with early versions from the fifteenth century (for example, Little Moreton Hall in Cheshire). This remained a popular way to extend the living space up to the eighteenth century.

The introduction of the chimney stack removed the need for a hall open to the roof, enabled the development of an upper floor and produced the consequent requirement for a staircase. From this time, kitchens in medium-sized houses, which previously had been in a separate building for fear of fire, were integrated into the main house and can often be identified by an extension or outshut added to an early dwelling (*see* Baigens Case Study in Chapter Three). There were still many small rural houses without chimney stacks during the sixteenth century; if a house was small and of inferior quality, it may have been demolished and a new house with an integral stack built in its place. After the demise of the single-height hall house, the basic house altered in size of plan, its number of storeys and in the position of key elements such as external doors, a chimney stack and staircase. Other than very regional solutions and a few local variations and houses built for specific purposes, small houses seem to fall into four main categories.

Cross-Passage House

Cross-passage houses are medieval in origin, but lasted until the eighteenth century in certain parts of the country. These houses are divided from front to back by a passage partitioning the interior space, with later versions having a fireplace attached to the dividing wall and named a 'hearth-passage'. They can be identified from outside by the position of the front door being slightly offset from the line of the stack. These houses can be two-bay in size or larger, sometimes with an additional stack on a side wall. The rural 'longhouse' and 'laithe house' are versions of this type.

Odiham, Hampshire (Grade II) *Now two cottages, the brick front on this timber-framed house has changed its appearance substantially. Lateral chimney-stacks have been added to the rear, turning the original hall into a two-storey house. The datable roof structure and plan indicate a mid fifteenth-century house, possibly of cross-passage design.*

Lobby-Entry or Baffle-Entry House

Lobby-entry or baffle-entry houses have two rooms and a loft above, with a chimney-stack

Dedham, Essex (Grade II) *These houses show a lobby entry (middle) with a further building at right angles (left) and a direct-entry property (right). All three have gabled gambrel roofs and, although updated in the eighteenth century, they may show evidence of earlier structures behind the brick.*

dividing the space, allowing one or two hearths in the middle of the house where the open hall fire would have been originally. The front door is in the centre of the façade, with the wall of the chimney stack close behind it producing a small lobby to hinder drafts and give access to each room. This house type can be clearly identified externally from the direct line between front door and chimney stack. When ladders became permanent staircases, an obvious position for them was tucked alongside the central stack or winding around it for support. In a three-bay version with a central stack, as can be seen at Pendean Farmhouse at the Weald & Downland Open Air Museum, illustrated later in this chapter, there would have been an unheated service room. As changes in living arrangements made this uncomfortable and possibly after the repeal of the Hearth Tax in 1689, additional stacks were often built on to outside walls to increase the number of hearths. Later, many new houses were built with one central and one lateral stack, forming another standard house type.

Direct-Entry House

Direct-entry houses have two living rooms, one of which is accessed straight from the front door, with a loft above. This type of house was built from the seventeenth to the nineteenth century. The arrangement includes a chimney or pair of chimneys on the side walls and dormer windows in the roof. There were various positions for the external doors and staircase, and later the height of the building increased to accommodate upstairs rooms rather than a loft.

Sherbourne, Gloucestershire *This late example of a direct-entry cottage is single storey with the roof space lit by gabled dormers. It was probably built in the nineteenth century of limestone and reclaimed materials in the form of an arched stone doorway.*

Emsworth, Hampshire (Grade II) A late eighteenth-century double-pile house seen from the side but designed to be viewed from the front, where expensive Flemish laid brick with blue headers has been used.

Double-Pile House

Double-pile houses are double-fronted dwellings of four rooms on each of two floors.

Double-pile single-fronted houses (also called two up two down) are half the size and lack the symmetry of the standard double pile. Built usually in pairs or rows, they are found in both rural and urban situations as at Lowndes Buildings in Farnham, Surrey. The introduction of this type in the middle to late eighteenth century saw the final development of the outshut.

Certain house types were designed and built to fulfil a specific role, such as longhouses in Devon, which were of cross-passage design to house people at one end and animals at the other, lower, end. These were usually built of stone, as were the similar Yorkshire examples, called laithe houses. Semi-fortified buildings, such as stone bastel houses found in the far north, had their living quarters raised to first-floor level with space for cattle below. Houses were also built to accommodate workrooms, such as weavers' cottages found in many parts of the country, examples existing from the seventeenth and eighteenth centuries in Corsham, Wiltshire, and in villages in North Yorkshire. Framework knitters' houses, defined by the large first floor or attic windows to maximize daylight working hours, can be found in Nottinghamshire and Leicestershire. These cottage industries gradually ceased to be viable as industrial-scale production took over in the nineteenth century.

Lettaford, Devon (Grade I) Once thatched, this granite longhouse has been restored and shows the original division of living quarters to the left and a shippon or barn for livestock to the right, divided by a wide cross passage. (By kind permission of the Landmark Trust)

Cromford, Derbyshire (Grade II*) This row of eleven textile workers' houses was built in 1776–77 by Thomas Arkright, the mill owner, for his workers and included continuous workshops on the top floor. The early fenestration of one fixed casement and one sash is the original design. (© M. Campbell Cole; reproduced by kind permission of the Landmark Trust)

The Formally Planned House

New small houses of the eighteenth century followed previously used ideas on the layout of internal space but, where influenced by contemporary fashions, looked to Georgian proportions and detailing. In fashionable houses fireplaces were by now always built on the side walls, allowing the position of the most important internal feature, the staircase, to dominate the central space. Designs for eighteenth- and nineteenth-century town houses were governed firstly by the large Georgian high-ceilinged terrace and later by the even more widespread Victorian variety, both influenced by the many architectural pattern books available during this time.

The small Victorian terraced house was built to a standard plan with positions for key

Bosham, West Sussex (Grade II) A good example of regional 'polite' architecture, Bell Cottage is single pile, extended at the rear to give an L-shape plan. Chimneys at each end, early sash windows and brick eaves' cornice all indicate that it was built in the eighteenth century.

Tettenhall, West Midlands (Grade II) The owners of this terrace of four double-pile houses (circa 1830) have not fallen into the trap of replacing their Georgian windows with large-paned sashes of the horned variety.

features that varied little across the country. The front door opened on to a hall, showing the staircase (a legacy from the Georgian period), with the main reception room accommodating the chimney stack on the party wall, enabling it to be shared with the house next door, often a mirror image of its neighbour on all floors. Smaller workers' houses, such as back-to-backs, courts (houses without direct street access) and

Ruddington, Nottinghamshire (Grade II) These four cottages, of which the middle two are back-to-back, were built in the early nineteenth century for framework knitters and their families working in the adjacent frameshop. (By kind permission of The Framework Knitters Museum)

early flats, were designed to minimum standards, usually with shared external sanitary arrangements and little or no other outside space. As small as one-up and one-down, the design of these houses had been condemned by local by-laws in many towns by the middle of the nineteenth century, although in some they continued to be built for another hundred years. By-law houses were the result of a number of national building acts and the local by-laws that were designed to enforce them. These acts stipulated the width of new streets, applied strict building standards and controlled such details as the heights of ceilings and, more than anything else, these acts shaped Victorian and Edwardian terraced housing. Bathrooms were introduced into the design of better houses from as early as the 1830s, but for smaller homes the perceived need for a separate internal space for washing was not recognized until the end of the nineteenth century.

By the turn of the twentieth century, many houses were being built for the aspiring middle classes on the outskirts of towns and cities on larger plots, allowing ground plans to be less restrictive. Flexibility in the internal layout, in keeping with the return to everything medieval, enabled the hall to become a pleasant wide area

Henley, Oxfordshire *Victorian terraces were built for a wide-ranging market and this one has features to indicate a superior version of around 1899, including stone banding and detailing around the doorway, terracotta brattishing on the ridge and a tiled pathway. Originally, the door may have been half-glazed to light the hallway and the fanlight is a painted imitation.*

Wolverhampton, West Midlands *This pair of villas forms part of a suburban avenue outside the city, built in 1911. Influences of the Arts and Crafts Movement can be seen both inside and outside, with this example echoing the 'Queen Anne' revival of the middle of the nineteenth century.*

rather than a corridor between the back and front doors. There was less of a fashion for symmetry in detached houses and only semis were required to be mirror images of each other. In a logical move to keep costs down, small groups of houses often shared common features and details although size might change, while in other types the plan might remain static and the detailing vary. From the Edwardian era to the 1930s, estates often had an eclectic mix of medieval half-timbering and Queen Anne within the same development (and sometimes the same house).

Four million houses were built between the two World Wars, many in suburbia in styles echoing the past, but a small number of houses appeared that were described as 'International Style'. Art Deco, as it was later termed, was epitomized by clean, simple designs, an abundance of light from large wrap-around windows and offered a new open-plan style of living. Most Art Deco houses were architect designed and commissioned, and one stunning monument to the style is 'Joldwyns', by Oliver Hill, situated in

Holmbury St Mary, Surrey. However, a few were built from a modest design featured in the Ideal Home Exhibition of 1934 (*see* Sunspan Case Study in Chapter Seven), and speculative builders added curved metal windows and stucco to their repertoire of features for semi-detached suburban houses.

The interwar years are also known for the large number of bungalows built in England. Although single-storey dwellings have their roots in English vernacular architecture, this version was imported from abroad. The term bungalow derived from 'bangalo', meaning a lightly built single-storey house from Bengal, and the first few were built in England in the middle of the nineteenth century. In 1908 the King had one built on the Sandringham estate, giving the style royal approval, pattern books started offering models and the bungalow is now part of England's architectural heritage.

Influences and Constraints

There were great changes in house design during the seventeenth and eighteenth centuries as classical influences from abroad started to filter through to medium and small houses. Speculative building initiated by such events as the Great Fire of London and guided, at least in

the capital, by early building acts and builders' pattern books, increased the populated areas around towns. Between 1700 and 1830 one million small houses were built. For the first time, certain senior craftsmen expanded their knowledge of world architecture, started drawing out ideas and began to practise as professional designers, calling themselves 'architects'. Changes in the status of the professional classes meant that they could afford to build elegant houses of medium size, such as Pallant House in Chichester, West Sussex (1713), built for Henry Peckham, a wealthy wine merchant, and

Farnham, Surrey (Grade II*) Built by Thomas Piggott, a London grocer, in the early eighteenth century on the site of the town's corn rooms, this house exemplifies 'polite' architecture built by wealthy merchants in towns across the country during this period.

Peppercombe, Devon Castle Bungalow was built of timber in the 1920s and was marketed through the pattern books of the company Boulton and Paul, which went on to build aircraft during the Second World War. (Reproduced by kind permission of the Landmark Trust)

Pattern book This design for a pair of Gothic-style single-storey model cottages for the working classes is by E.L. Tarbuck (circa 1860). In the style of early almshouses, the dwellings had the luxury of an inside toilet.

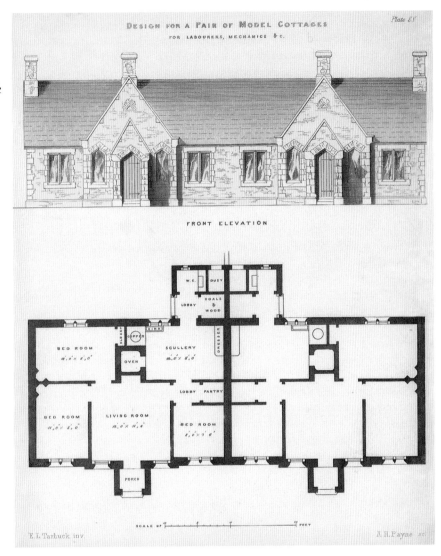

Pattern Books

Publications on European architecture were produced in England from the sixteenth century. By early in the eighteenth century these influences were being distilled into a range of inspiring and informative books designed for the average builder who required some interpretation of the

Pickford House in Derby, built by a local architect, Joseph Pickford, in 1770 for his own occupation.

theories of classical architecture. Batty Langley, a carpenter, surveyor and landscape gardener, produced the first architectural pattern book in 1726, and, over a period of twenty years, produced many volumes on surveying, building and gardening. Builders could consult on all forms of detailing and interior design in such publications as Langley's *The City and Country Builder's and Workman's Treasury of Design*, published in 1741. Some more academic writers of the time disliked the simple interpretations offered by Langley and derogatory phrases such as 'Batty

Langley Gothic' were coined as a result. Pattern books of the first half of the eighteenth century concentrated on practical building issues, but by the middle of the century drawings showing a range of styles were available. William Halfpenny was almost as prolific as Langley and included designs based on oriental and Gothic styles. His *Rural Architecture in the Chinese Taste* was published in 1755 and was clearly not aimed at the average cottage owner, but at the wealthy landowner with an interest in 'Chinoiserie'.

A number of prominent architects produced pattern books and manuals to help with the rebuilding and housing of the poor. John Wood the younger, of Bath fame, published his *Series of Plans for Cottages of Habitations of the Labourer* in 1781, the first pattern book of workers' cottages, produced in an attempt to encourage landowners to improve the living conditions of their tenants. This idea was perpetuated by John Claudius Loudon with his *Encyclopaedia of Cottage, Farm and Villa Architecture* of 1833, and by this time estate villages were being designed and built in the picturesque style. Pattern books helped shape many model villages, as at Blaise Hamlet near Bristol, circa 1780. These and other philanthropic efforts were fuelled by such publications as

Robert Owen's plans for 'alternative communities' (1813), catering for working mothers, and Banister Fletcher's *Model Houses for the Industrial Classes*, published in 1871. In addition to pattern books showing plans and elevations, makers produced books of their designs, one of the first being Thomas Chippendale, whose catalogues, such as *The Gentleman & Cabinet-maker's Director* of 1754, were as much used as pattern books from which to copy designs as they were for selling furniture. Catalogues containing metalwork, plasterwork and other decorative detailing were available and all helped to determine the way houses looked.

Revivals of Styles

Various house styles, proliferated through pattern books, were built across the country at varying times throughout the eighteenth and nineteenth century, starting with large houses and in time influencing medium and smaller homes where owners could afford to rebuild or improve their properties. The Palladian Revival shaped the look of much eighteenth-century housing, along with more general classical styling of the time. The Gothic Revival, or 'Gothick' (sometimes used to distinguish it from the original period), was popular in the late eighteenth century, inspired by such eccentrics as Horace Walpole, a pioneer in

Blaise Hamlet, Bristol (Grade I) *Circular Cottage (1812) in the 'cottage orné' style is one of a group of thatched cottages around a central green designed by John Nash for the retired workers of the nearby Blaise Castle. (By kind permission of The National Trust)*

Portsmouth, Hampshire *This small Regency villa was built around 1840 and includes castellated towers as well as Gothic arched windows.*

Albury, Surrey (Grade II) *Converted from shops to houses, this nineteenth-century row is an imitation of the medieval, and manages, in its enthusiasm, to include every element of period detailing. The façade incorporates mock Tudor half-timbering, fishtail tile hanging, bargeboards, Gothic arches, casement windows and gabled dormers all under a roof dominated by a collection of huge decorated chimney-stacks.*

its use. Taking a small seventeenth-century house called Strawberry Hill in Twickenham, London, Walpole rebuilt it over a period of a quarter of a century, adding a medieval tower, battlements and moulded chimneys, with the result that the phrase 'Strawberry Hill Gothic' was conceived. The fashion for Gothic architecture continued for much of the nineteenth century, influenced by fictional writing and the Victorian romantic ideal. It appealed to public ecclesiastical leanings, but was

only one of the house types fashionable during the Victorian period, as industrial processes allowed more freedom to experiment with materials and detailing. In the middle of the century there was a mixture of motifs and many average builders, with little contextual knowledge or understanding of early practices, used every opportunity and every style to embellish and decorate. The nineteenth century included half-timbering, herringbone brickwork, leaded lights, tile-hung façades and tall chimneys, sometimes all on the same house.

It was not until the Arts and Crafts Movement was established towards the end of the century that there was a true understanding of the methods and a return to the practices of medieval building. In its 'purist' form, this led to the building of vernacular stone cottages in the country, made inconspicuous by their use of local material and style, as was built by Ernest Gimson in Leicestershire. More ambitious architects of the movement combined modern methods and medieval influences, building both on urban and rural plots. Between 1900 and the Second World War the ethos of the Arts and Crafts Movement was turned into a pastiche called Tudoresque. It was created out of a romantic vision of the past that had little to do with traditional building and everything to do with the provision of houses for an expanding population.

Acts and Taxes

Houses have been shaped not only by positive influences from home and abroad and by innovative building technology, but also by restrictive acts and punitive taxes. Taxes, often property or land-based using tithe or feudal systems, had been collected from the Middle Ages, with certain periods in history calling for greater taxation, such as during wars. After the restoration of the monarchy in 1660, when the country was almost bankrupted by the debts of the Civil War and Cromwell's Commonwealth, a number of new taxes were devised. One of these, the hearth tax, was collected on the basis of the number of

Grayshott, Surrey *A more subtle approach on this house built in 1929, with Tudorbethan half-timbering on the façade and tile hanging on the rear.*

hearths in a house, which impacted on house design from 1662 to 1689. After the first year, around a quarter of the population, in poorer dwellings, became exempt. It also led to some new homes being built with many more chimney stacks than hearths, indicating either forward planning or a desire to appear wealthy without incurring greater cost. This tax was difficult to collect as it required access to the house to make an assessment, so one of the first changes William and Mary made on coming to the throne in 1689 was to abolish the hearth tax and introduce a poll tax, which proved equally unpopular.

From the late seventeenth century through the eighteenth there were a number of other innovative ways to increase the coffers, including the window tax that was started in 1696 to help offset high inflation and the cost of various military campaigns. Through many revisions this tax remained until the reign of Queen Victoria 150 years later, but, though often described as 'the tax on light and air', it was generally only levied on houses with more than six windows. This tax, with its many increases, had a profound impact on the external appearance of new houses, of which there were many during this period. New house designs and technological advances in glassmaking produced a conflict between enjoying these innovations and the expense of implementing them. With the addition of a tax on glass (imposed in 1746), one way to reduce the impact of both taxes to block up a number of windows. After its repeal, or as finances improved, these windows were more than likely reopened, often making it difficult to confirm that the tax was responsible for existing blanks in a building. In 1784 a brick and tile tax was introduced to help pay for the recent War of Independence in America, but, despite increases

Stanton in the Peak, Derbyshire (Grade II*) Holly House had, until very recent alterations, eight blocked up windows on its façade, making it a likely example of window tax evasion. An estate house, it was built in the late seventeenth century but refronted shortly after, making the reason for the blocked windows still speculative. The choice of replacement windows on this important house during recent renovations seems strange, as the six sashes are not original and they appear to have wooden, rather than stone mullions, with sashes rather than casements.

Tenterden, Kent (Grade II) Craythorne House, circa 1790, is a timber-framed house with wooden boarding cut to imitate stone. It shows many classical features such as a pedimented window and doorcase (on the façade, not shown), wooden cornice and keystones. The choice of materials may have been intended to avoid the brick tax.

in the tax in 1794 and again in 1803, building in brick continued to expand as few alternatives were either available or deemed appropriate. By 1851 all taxes affecting house design had been repealed.

Acts of Parliament altered house design in the town and the country, both to reduce the risk of fire and the spread of disease and to establish good working practices. As early as the sixteenth century there were attempts to control building, and a spate of town fires in the late sixteenth and early seventeenth century led to some measures being taken. Tiverton in Devon was the subject of two fires in 1598 and 1612. It was believed that the wrath of God had been brought upon the town by having a market day on Monday and therefore requiring preparation to be undertaken on the Sabbath. This led to a charter being set up and the market day was changed, but by the next fire in 1731 it was perhaps clear that building design was the more likely culprit. Some attempt was made during the reign of James I to set and control standards for building, including the banning of the jetty in the City of London due to a perceived risk of fire with these particular buildings as they reduced the distance across the street. Despite many devastating fires in towns across the country it was not until after the 1666 Great Fire of London that legislation concentrated on minimizing the risk of fire from overcrowding. The London Building Act of 1667 extended earlier controls in the use of building materials and styles and introduced building inspectors to oversee the rebuilding of the city.

Despite many other English towns suffering similar drastic fires, the regulations laid down in London were not adopted in some county towns for another fifty to 100 years. Bristol clearly attempted some early measures to control fires, including a curfew (meaning to extinguish the hearth fire) of 9pm at night for homes, and, as a result of a destructive fire in 1647, issuing fire buckets to council members. There were further fire-prevention initiatives in London that affected the design of houses. In 1707 wooden decoration like eaves cornices were forbidden on the exterior of new houses and an act of 1709 altered the façade further by insisting that all windows be recessed from the front of the brick or stonework by 4 inches, a restriction that lasted nearly 200 years (*see* Mayburys Case Study in Chapter Two).

In the eighteenth century there were further fires across the country and the face of Dorchester, for example, was changed forever by three fires. Although the London acts only applied to the capital, they had by now been taken by many places as examples for local by-laws. In 1774 the next London Building Act had a significant effect on house design as it attempted to standardize new town houses, determining size, layout and price according to the street width, and it was the final word in town fire prevention. The Public Health and Building Acts of 1848 and 1875 tackled the requirements for water supply, drainage, waste disposal and refuse collection. By 1868 there was increased power for local authorities to control slums. The Act of 1875 laid down standards for both layout and construction, and houses built after this act are often called By-law houses. The Housing of the Working Classes Act of 1889 accelerated the process of change, so that by the First World War the building of small, tightly packed terraces in industrial towns had ceased.

The Beginning of Speculative Building

Speculative building was undertaken by a range of different types of people, from wealthy landowners, leasing land to people with money to invest, to early building companies. The construction of groups of houses by speculative builders became established in London after the Great Fire in 1666 and the majority of Georgian houses in the capital were built in this way. Often the principal developer would draw up plans for the overall architectural scheme of the square or terrace and sell plots to a number of smaller builders, who undertook to build a number of houses within the scheme and to adhere to the exterior design. This pattern of building spread to provincial towns like Bath and Bristol

Southsea, Hampshire (Grade II) *Sussex Terrace, built around 1850, is the crowning glory of Thomas Ellis Owen's speculative building in Southsea.*

and can be seen in most other towns to a lesser extent. Speculators in the nineteenth century, such as Thomas Cubitt in London, Thomas Kemp in Brighton, Richard Grainger in Newcastle and Thomas Ellis Owen in Portsmouth, all left their mark on the area they developed.

Houses have always been attached together in densely populated areas to utilize space and materials. Influenced by the Italian piazza, attached houses started to be built encircling a piece of open ground, the original design for Covent Garden (1631) being one of the earliest and most famous examples. Further out of London, the earliest existing speculatively built group of attached houses is at Newington Green (1658) in the once small rural village of Islington. The first term used to describe these houses was a 'row', as at Minor Canon Row in Rochester (1736), and, in the Netherlands, attached properties are still described as 'English Row Houses'. This term was superseded by the word 'terrace', which originally referred to a raised piece of ground, but when houses were built as at Adelphi Terrace (started 1768) on an elevated platform alongside the Thames in London, the term was transferred to the houses. The word terrace is now associated both with the elegant Georgian terraces of London and Bath and with the back-to-back rows of the Victorian era, built cheaply in all the major towns and cities but particularly in the north.

As the nineteenth-century terraces sprang up everywhere to house the growing urban population, the upper-class terrace of the previous century was still sheltering within enclosed parks and communal gardens. London estates were enclosed with railings, as at Bedford Square (1775), the most well-preserved Georgian example, and the whole of the Bedford Estate was gated until the late nineteenth century. The Royal Crescent in Bath (started 1767) is a terrace built on a raised area. It shows classical influences from grand buildings such as palaces and presents a unified composition. In the Georgian terrace the façades of the individual houses were identical and it was the effect of the

Bath, Somerset (Grade I) The Circus was built in the 1750s by John Wood the Younger to his father's design and overlooks a central communal garden. Thomas Gainsborough the painter and William Pitt both lived in the terrace.

grand overall design that was of primary importance.

In London this concept fitted in well with the 1774 Building Act, which identified four rates of terraced housing, the designs of which were to be used for all new building in the capital. The act stipulated structural details and each house was defined by size, cost and external details, such as appropriate positions of windows, and with the fashionable leaning towards simple façades the cheaper rate houses presented a uniformity not seen on this scale at any time in the past. The largest 'first rate' house was usually a three-bay of four storeys and up to 24ft (7.3m) wide. The 'second rate' house was a narrower two-bay with four storeys, the 'third rate' property narrower still, with the 'fourth rate' being no more than 12ft (3.7m) wide. The rigidity of these stipulations and the current fashion for simplicity gave rise to many identical façades, although, once inside, the interiors were individual in design and lavish in style. There were exceptions to uniform façades, as can be seen on temple- or palace-fronted designs, where the middle and ends of the terrace were given prominence with columns, pilasters and pediments, and it was these 'feature units' in the terrace that were the more highly sought after.

Pattern book The plan
and elevation of a pair of
'third rate' semi-detached
cottages of 1860, show
considerable exterior
detailing such as stucco,
quoins and pedimented
windows.

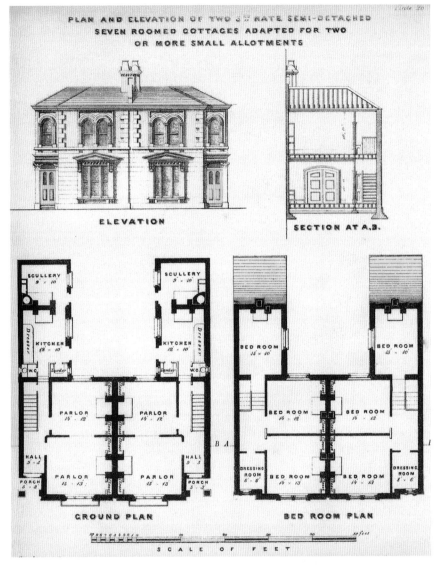

By the early nineteenth century, influences
from the Middle and Far East created what we
now call the 'Regency' style, which was a wel-
come change to what had perhaps become a
somewhat severe classically influenced house
style with little opportunity for personal ideas
from either builder or client. However, it is
largely superficial additions to the basic structure that identifies a Regency terrace from its
predecessors. As most towns had a foundry by
this time, both wrought and cast iron were used
for balconies, staircases, railings and in some

cases windows. Brighton Pavilion is a monument
to this style and to the technical innovations of
its time. Regency terraces often still had a sense
of symmetry, although houses were generally
narrower than earlier in the century, with later
Regency houses being between 16ft (5m) and
19ft (5.8m) wide. Spa towns, such as Brighton,
Leamington and Cheltenham, which were popular during this period, have many versions of
Regency houses, epitomizing the 'frivolous'
nature of this era. Some speculative developers
did not exercise the level of control that was

Ramsgate, Kent (Grade II) *Guildford Lawn (the term 'lawn' used in this town and in Cheltenham), built around 1842, is an elegant row of nineteen Regency houses on two sides of a square.*

Bosham, West Sussex *This Victorian row of possible coastguard cottages is double pile in plan and may once have included another cottage on the left to balance the façade.*

required to produce a unified group of houses and Spencer Square in Ramsgate, built from 1820 until the 1840s, although attractive in parts, is clearly the victim of speculative building that took too long from inception to completion.

Victorian terraces seem to fall into two categories, the basic lower-class dwelling found in inner-city areas and a more ornate version further out into the suburbs and in towns. The better quality terraces were designed using the mass of pattern books available and were built, usually of quality brick, with detailing of stone, cast iron and stained glass. Due to published designs, improved transport and a general rise in individual wealth these properties can be found all over the country. The building of fashionable houses by wealthy merchants in villages surrounding major towns was common by the eighteenth century. The wholesale transformation of outlying villages into suburbs in the nineteenth century started with speculators building superior terraces and semi-detached Gothic and Italianate villas for the growing middle classes. This exodus from cities was made easier as new improved public transport methods were introduced in the form of horse-drawn omnibuses and electric tramcars, both of which were used in Leeds in the 1890s and were pivotal in the development of Roundhay and Headingley as suburbs. Eventually, this housing need led to the development of the 'garden suburb', a term coined in the 1870s with the building of the Bedford Park Estate, London in Queen Anne style, followed by Letchworth in 1904 and by Hampstead Garden Suburb in London shortly after.

In contrast, cheap workers' housing, although it had been in existence from the early days of the Industrial Revolution in certain areas of large towns, was built on a massive scale in the Victorian period. Long Row in Nostell, West Yorkshire, a terrace of forty-seven miners' cottages built by Charles Winn, and Silkstone Row in Lower Altofts in Yorkshire, with over sixty dwellings in an 800ft (244m) terrace, were both built in the 1860s. In many cheaply built terraces, dwellings were built back-to-back, which made the most of common walls and shared chimney stacks to reduce the cost of construction, but with a health cost to those who had to live in them. While some landowners had been improving the life of rural tenants since the eighteenth century, the living conditions of workers in towns were unregulated and squalid. They only began to improve with the nineteenth-century Public Health and Building Acts, instigated by the death of Prince Albert from cholera, which required private landlords and builders to adhere to certain minimum standards. These Victorian statutes were more about improving conditions than having a direct impact upon house design, as it became clear that it was the density of Victorian housing, rather than the design, that needed to change. This issue was addressed by a breed of enlightened philanthropists, who designed not only new housing for the working population, but also modelled for them a new existence.

Model Towns and Villages

There had been a great many towns and villages designed and built for a specific purpose between the seventeenth and the twentieth centuries. Sometimes this was a philanthropic gesture on the part of a landowner, but often it was a desire to demolish the existing village to make way for a new landscaping plan for the big house and its surrounding park. This activity was called emparking and was widespread across England due to the influence of gardeners such as Lancelot 'Capability' Brown. Earlier settlements were erased and villagers, if they were lucky, were rehoused in picturesque cottages that improved the landowner's view, as at Milton Abbas in Dorset, started in 1773. However, the eighteenth century also saw a rise in the conscience of landowners in their moral responsibility to their workers and many new villages were built with churches, schools and inns, as at Sledmere, Yorkshire, which was started in the middle of the eighteenth century.

Villages and towns were built to house workers engaged in industry and Whitehaven in Cumbria is said to have been the first, built around 1680 by Sir John Lowther as a coal-exporting town and the first English example of a Renaissance style of street planning outside London. Canal- and sea-based villages were built, such as Mistley in Essex in 1768, and Shadlow in Derbyshire a decade later.

Religious and charitable trusts were involved in providing decent housing for the poor in cities. One such organization was the Society for Improving the Conditions of the Labouring Classes, and its first block of family houses was completed in Bloomsbury in 1850. An

Derby, Derbyshire (Grade II) As part of the first railway village, this house on North Street, built in 1842, was the most basic two-up, two-down version (see Railway Cottages Case Study).

American, George Peabody, founded the Peabody Trust in 1862, building five estates in London in the first decade of its building programme, with many more since, keeping true to its doctrine for nearly 150 years. In 1884–85 The Royal Commission on the Housing of the Working Classes published a report highlighting the conditions of housing for the poor. That, and further studies showing the situation to be worsening, provided the impetus for a group of later villages and gave rise to a new pattern of workers' villages away from cities and into suburbs.

The Industrial Revolution and the Enclosure Acts altered the pattern of habitation in England

Edensor, Derbyshire (Grade II) In 1838, having removed the original village, which was too close to Chatsworth, the sixth Duke of Devonshire hired Joseph Paxton, his landscape gardener, to design the layout of Edensor with the help of a draughtsman from the office of J.C. Loudon. Using Loudon's pattern book, cottages were built in gritstone with Italianate windows, Jacobean gables, bargeboards and Tudor chimneys.

and produced overcrowding in the larger towns and cities, to which people migrated in search of employment. A number of industrialists recognized the poor quality of life and short life expectancy of many low-paid workers and as a response created new towns and villages. Saltaire, outside Bradford, mainly built between 1852 and 1872, is one of the famous models of workers' villages, consisting of 820 stone houses with Italian-style detailing. For his workers the mill owner, Sir Titus Salt, not only built houses, but also created a whole new lifestyle, containing all the elements needed for a healthy and

happy existence, although he did not see fit to include a public house. Status within the workforce determined the size of house, and a basic workman's cottage consisted of a cellar, pantry, living room, scullery and three bedrooms. In addition to these basics, overlookers had a parlour, washroom and up to six bedrooms, depending on the size of their family, but even the smallest three-bedroom home must have been impressive compared to the industrial slums of the time.

There is sense of a return to the medieval feudal system, with the lord of the manor providing shelter for his workers, and the scheme at Saltaire was only one of a growing number of purpose-built villages in the optimistic and prosperous Victorian age. In the 1880s George Cadbury designed and began building Bournville Village near Birmingham, which later became known as 'the factory in the garden'. To develop the sense of community it was intended that Cadbury's workers should occupy only half of the 300 homes and, influenced by the Arts and Crafts Movement, there was a mixture of terraces and semis. Gardens were seen as important aspects of the village and Cadbury encouraged the growing of fruit and vegetables, as well as offering gardening support in the form of lectures and classes at the community hall. The soap manufacturer William Lever's version of the ideal village is called Port Sunlight (1890) and it consists of picturesque Tudor-style houses, while Joseph Rowntree's efforts were similarly successful at New Earswick in Yorkshire in 1902, which was described as a garden village. The architects Parker and Unwin of New Earswick later went on to design the garden cities of Letchworth and Welwyn, but these were speculative ventures aimed at middle-class professionals.

House Updating

Though there was a vast amount of new building during the Georgian and Victorian periods, many houses, though apparently of these periods, were originally timberframed or early stone

Bournville, West Midlands (Grade II) The brick villas, built by Joseph Cadbury for his workers, were designed with a number of architectural motifs, including crow-stepped gables, Venetian windows and Tudor-style half-timbering.

new façade in place of an earlier timber-frame structure and incorporating the new sash style of windows was a common practice, sometimes retaining the original low-ceilinged rooms and so creating strange full-length windows of squat proportions. For small houses it was often too costly to move the central chimney stack and this is a clear indicator of an earlier building, as a true Georgian house would have the fireplaces at the sides. The most frequent change was to the covering material on the roof and many period houses, originally thatched, were later given tiles or slates, which is clearly seen by the unnecessarily steep roof pitch.

External influences such as Acts of Parliament and taxes also had their effect on the way houses were altered, just as they did on the building of new properties, and windows are the most obvious feature to have been influenced by both. The updating of houses into more fashionable dwellings often occurred simultaneously within a town or village at times when the local industry was experiencing increased trade, but there are also towns that have retained early vernacular architecture as a result of a downturn in prosperity. In some cases, where the owners' personal wealth had increased considerably, they

structures that have been altered and updated over several centuries. Alterations to houses usually coincided with an increase in the status and wealth of the owner, or perhaps were linked to the next generation taking over the household. Heirs of large country houses often liked to alter and make fashionable the family seat, so the assumption is that this also happened to some degree in smaller properties, although evidence of why updating occurred at a particular time and under which owner is usually harder to find.

The largest period of updating seems to have been during the reigns of the four Georges, when many houses acquired fashionable details. A

Slindon, West Sussex (Grade II) Originally a lobby-entry house of three bays, additions on either side extended the property and a further period of gentrification took place in 1694, when the eaves cornice was added and sash windows replaced the earlier casements. The left-hand addition appears to have been a separate dwelling at this time.

could afford to demolish, ignore or convert their previous house to another use and build new. The Enclosure Acts (circa 1750–1830) not only changed the layout of the land, but also the use of farm buildings. Farmhouses were initially built in villages due to the scattered field strips of early agricultural land. However, with changes in land ownership many farmers vacated their out-of-date village houses (often turning them into a row of workers' cottages), and had a more prestigious house built elsewhere. A long, low continuous roof with one original chimney stack can often identify these adapted cottages. In the twentieth century, with the change to a more mechanized system of farming, many farmworkers' cottages have been sold and sometimes turned back into one house again.

The Moving of Houses

Many large, important period houses have been demolished in the last 100 years and it is impossible to estimate how many smaller ones have also disappeared. As late as the 1930s period houses could be demolished or moved without special permission, although some houses had a lucky escape. The Ancient House in Clare, Suffolk, built in 1473 (*see* Chapter Three) was due to be removed to America in the 1930s

Alwalton, Cambridgeshire (Grade II*) Lynch Lodge is a seventeenth-century rebuilt limestone porch, complete with Tuscan columns on the ground floor and Ionic ones above. (© D. Brabbs; reproduced by kind permission of The Landmark Trust)

Stoke by Nayland, Suffolk Originally a lobby-entry house (identified by the large central stack), it was divided into four cottages in the eighteenth century, a further stack built on to one end and Victorian bay windows inserted into the façade.

until it was rescued by a thoughtful local farmer. Many other structures and interiors found their way across the Atlantic before legislation was passed to halt the practice, for example the Elizabethan interiors of Flemings Hall in Suffolk. Although the moving of buildings from their regional context is not ideal, it can be the only way to save them if there is a scheduled change in the use of land or a road-building scheme. There is a long tradition of moving houses to new sites, either by careful demolition and re-erection, or by moving them intact, and there are examples such as at Newport on the Isle of Wight where a house was moved on rollers in the thirteenth century. In Cambridgeshire, Lynch Lodge started life as part of Chesterton House, a Jacobean stone property. When that house was demolished in 1807 a section of the house was dismantled and rebuilt at Alwalton.

As town centres started to be redeveloped in the Victorian period, early buildings were demolished or moved, made possible by the 1852 Act of Parliament to improve the flow of traffic through towns. Timber-framed houses are ideal, by their very design, for dismantling and re-erecting elsewhere. Grange Court, a timber-framed house in Leominster, was built in 1633, dismantled in 1855, sold at auction and rebuilt. It became the council offices in the late 1930s and narrowly missed being dismantled again for

Birmingham, West Midlands (Grade II) *Old Selly Manor is a fourteenth-century building that was moved half a mile (0.8km) to its present site by George Cadbury as part of Bournville. Its re-erection was completed in 1917.*

Singleton, West Sussex *Like all the buildings at this museum, Pendean was moved from its original position for its own protection. An early seventeenth-century lobby-entry, three-bay farmhouse, the rebuilding allows it to be seen as it would have been when first built. (By kind permission of The Weald & Downland Open Air Museum)*

Mersham, Kent (Grade II) Bridge House, a seventeenth-century timber-framed lobby-entry house, refaced later in brick, was jacked up and moved 180yd (55m) away from the main line of the Channel Tunnel rail link in 2000. (Reproduced by kind permission of Abbey Pynford Ltd)

export to America. Selly Manor House, of the early fourteenth century with Tudor additions, and Minworth Greaves, dating from the thirteenth century, were both moved by George Cadbury to Bournville Village in 1912. During the 1960s and 1970s a number of open-air museums were started, with the aim of saving threatened buildings. Properties were given to these museums and funds raised to dismantle and re-erect them on the museum site; such museums are an excellent place to begin when looking at architectural history. Moving complete houses is still being undertaken as expansions in transport networks require sections of land to be cleared.

Reclamation and its Effect on House Design

Evidence of the reuse of materials for building new structures can be found firstly in early churches, where Roman bricks and tiles were reused in Saxon and Norman buildings. Demolished Roman walls were also seen as useful stores of stone, as at the Vicar's Pele at Corbridge, Northumberland, a fourteenth-century Bastel Tower house, built with stone from a nearby Roman fort. Until the nineteenth

century, building materials were expensive and in some cases scarce, so reclamation was sensible. There is a mass of evidence of 500 years of reclamation in various periods, particularly during the Reformation in the sixteenth century and the Civil War a century later, and there are a vast number of houses that boast elements of earlier buildings within them. Recognizing a piece of material that is wrong for the age of the property is sometimes very obvious, as at Brixworth Church in Northants, where the brick arches contain narrow Roman tiles in a largely stone structure. However, there is much speculation surrounding pieces of building that may have come from elsewhere, especially when several centuries have passed and when the material has been reused many times. The foundations of Nonsuch, the grandest of all of Henry VIII's palaces, were partly built from the dismantled stone of Merton Priory in Surrey during the 1540s. The palace itself was dismantled during the late seventeenth century and the keeper of the Palace acquired some of the materials, including Tudor statuary and panels, to rebuild his own house in the 1680s. This house, called Durdans, was destroyed by fire in 1764, but foundations incorporating Merton stone, taken from Nonsuch, still exist in the new house on the site. Pitt Place in Epsom is also reputed to have reclaimed materials from Durdans incorporated into its structure. It is believed that some of the decorative interior panels from Nonsuch ended up at Loseley House in Surrey, but, as the whereabouts of much of the material is still unknown, the basic brick and stonework could be hidden in many standard buildings around the locality.

In more modest building projects, when new houses were built close to an earlier house, the materials were often reused and blocks of stone or good structural timbers were rarely wasted. Almost every owner of a timber-framed house will be able to identify a piece of wood with unnecessary joint cuts, indicating that it may have started life elsewhere. Most types of stone are very durable and, depending on the location and carved detail, can be expensive, and it is for

Salisbury, Wiltshire (Grade I) The use of thin clay tiles on this early fourteenth-century structure is unusual in a county renowned for stone. The tiles were probably reclaimed, as the walls are built in a very random way and there is no evidence of the use of the tiles for pattern value.

these reasons that reclaimed stone is often found in new situations. During the Dissolution of the Monasteries, which started in 1536 and gathered pace in 1539, much good-quality stonework became available for reuse. Many new owners of these lands and buildings did nothing with them until some thirty years later, when, with the Catholic Mary Tudor dead, they were sure no reprisals would occur. The building material was either sold off to others or used to rebuild a dwelling on the existing site. Titchfield Abbey in Hampshire was one of the first to be

converted into a house, using stone from the monastery and adding brick chimneys and fireplaces. It became Place House in 1542, only to be demolished by another generation 250 years later, and the materials used a third time to extend another property nearby.

Another opportunity for acquiring building materials came during the Civil War, when large houses and castles were slighted by Parliamentary troops. The large Elizabethan brick building of Basing House, near Basingstoke in Hampshire, was one such casualty. The massive number of bricks available when the house was reduced to rubble must have gone somewhere, and some of the houses in the village appear to have been built of quality brick of the right age.

Sometimes there is clear documentary evidence of reclamation, as in the exploits of Sir Clough Williams-Ellis, the creator of Portmeirion in Wales. In larger houses, documents can prove not only the alterations over the centuries, but also the purchasing of parts of other houses. In 1786 Montecute House in Somerset, an Elizabethan building, resited a stone porch rescued from the sixteenth-century Clifton Maybank in Dorset after it had been partially dismantled. Smaller projects also have their examples in the past. The Vyne, a house of Tudor origin near Basingstoke in Hampshire, had one owner in the 1840s who moved fire

Wherwell, Hampshire This garden wall is made from flints and reclaimed sections of dressed stone from old Wherwell church, demolished in 1858.

Titchfield, Hampshire *Stone from this thirteenth-century abbey was reused, with the addition of brick, to convert the building into a house, but the stone is also likely to be found in smaller properties in the village. (By kind permission of English Heritage)*

***Old Basing, Hampshire
(Grade II)** Locally made red
bricks, laid in mostly English
bond, were used to build this
seventeenth-century house;
bricks reclaimed from Basing
House, which was reduced to
rubble in 1645, may have
been used.*

***Portmeirion, Wales.** Clough Williams-Ellis was an early conservator of ruined buildings and he rebuilt them in
this village (1925–75), as a collection of architectural parts from several centuries, countries and architects in a
wonderful eclectic mix.*

Lavenham, Suffolk (Grade I) *If it wasn't for the 1920s restoration of the right-hand section of this house, its fifteenth-century timber-framed structure may not have been apparent under eighteenth-century gentrification.*

surrounds and panelling from one room to another and created library shelves out of pews from the local parish church, but thankfully all his efforts were well-documented.

The Arts and Crafts Movement, with its love of the medieval, promoted an interest in using not only reclaimed building materials, but also whole buildings. The expert way in which medieval barns were grafted on to existing houses is often very convincing, and only the well-kept documentation and oral history identify them as reclaimed buildings. One of the best examples is Great Dixter, East Sussex, by Edwin Lutyens, who was an advocate of reclamation, although not to the extent of other lesser known Arts and Crafts architects. Detmar Blow built Little Ridge in 1903 using the shell of an early seventeenth-century stone manor house. Extended and renamed, it escaped the notice of the local conservation team and in 1972 the owners were granted permission to demolish it.

Despite rudimentary building regulations brought in during the seventeenth century, until the survey of England's buildings was started in the late 1940s owners were fairly free to alter, adapt and demolish houses at will. Early alterations, and the difficulty in enforcing listed building legislation, has led to hoards of historic

building materials being on the market, the provenance of which is very often unknown. Reclamation is now big business and with much legal and illegal removing of architectural features it seems set to continue. In 1971 over 90,000 houses were demolished in England and Wales, with presumably at least some of these having been built in the nineteenth century and with some materials having a resale value. Revivals in styles can be confusing when looking at and dating buildings, but the reuse of materials is even more confusing to all but professional architectural historians. As period home owners become more conscious of historical detail, and if when reinstating lost features they choose to buy reclaimed, it will be increasingly difficult to identify original features unless documentary evidence is kept.

As an example of good practice that owners should look at is the complete restoration of Uppark House in West Sussex. The National Trust restored the house after a devastating fire in 1989, using the wealth of British skill in the conservation and craft fields. For the replacement of lost items, remaking features is the safest way to ensure that craft skills are perpetuated and that the market for stolen or inadvisably removed period features dwindles.

Northiam, East Sussex (Grade I) *Great Dixter, a mid fifteenth-century manor house, was enlarged in 1911 by the addition of a derelict sixteenth-century hall house (on the right) rebuilt on the site.*

Heacham, Norfolk (Grade II) *The section of this house on the right is an unassuming late Georgian brick house. The late nineteenth-century Gothic stone tower has within it a number of medieval ecclesiastical stones, possibly from the nearby church.*

CASE STUDY:

Description

This early railway development comprises of three adjoining roads and two culs-de-sac. The majority of houses are of two storeys with substantial cellars, as at Railway Terrace. They originally consisted of a hall and three rooms on each floor, but in the last century the upstairs plan was altered to provide a bathroom. The rest of the development is made up of smaller, simpler houses found in North Street (now called Calvert) and larger double-fronted properties in Leeds Place and elsewhere. All the houses were built of light-red brick in Flemish bond, and those on Railway Terrace and Midland Place have stone banding at first-floor level and a parapet above a brick dentil cornice showing a simple classical influence which echoed the original station. This detailing also appears on the large central chimney stack that pierces the slate roof, with

Location: Derbyshire

Date: 1842

Type: Victorian railway cottages (Grade II)

a smaller stack to the rear (allowing for a fireplace in every room).

During the 1960s and 1970s this area suffered deterioration and, as a result, some of the interior detailing was lost. During the restoration period in the following decade architectural detailing was retained, such as

RAILWAY COTTAGES

balusters, cornicing and four-panelled doors. Externally, all the properties have the original company paintwork colour and the scheme is completed by traditional street lighting.

History

North Midland Railway was probably the first company to build a railway 'village' of this kind. The company employed the architect Francis Thompson to design the scheme, which consisted of a station (the original has since been demolished), the Midland Hotel, ninety-two houses, four shops and a commercial inn. The design created three main streets, North Street, Midland Place and Railway Terrace (spelling out the company name) and added two culs-de-sac, Leeds Place and Sheffield Place, naming the two main termini. There were seventeen different house designs, ranging from two-up, two-down to the large double-fronted versions for senior employees, including the stationmaster, whose house was Number Two, Midland Place.

In 1979 a grant from the Architectural Heritage Fund made possible the restoration of some of these properties (some had already been demolished and others lost as part of the plan to create contemporary amenities and a greater sense of space for the retained properties). Other than two large properties at the end, much of Leeds Place was demolished to create a curved cul-de-sac with parking places for the residents of Sheffield Place. The overall scheme reduced the flow of traffic to the area and created small front gardens for the Railway Terrace houses by moving the main road a few feet, a change of which The Midland Railway Horticultural and Cottage Garden Society of 1885 would have approved.

Most of the houses have paired doorways with elaborate doorcases of stone and include a step leading to a four-panelled door with a five-paned overdoor light. The well-proportioned sash windows and the doorways are completed with rubbed brick arches.

The scheme included this butcher's shop at the end of North Street (now a house), a grocer at the original Number Two, Railway Terrace (since demolished) and a bakery and general store in other parts of the scheme.

The houses on Railway Terrace probably would have been categorized as 'third rate' (as determined by the 1774 London Building Act). They included a signalling-style alarm system attached under the eaves to wake householders for their shift.

The Ordnance Survey map of 1852 depicts the original layout of the railway village, showing a communal garden with a rope walk, which by 1881 had become a less enticing area of toilet blocks.

Description

This leafy suburb of Wolverhampton is home to a collection of nineteen detached early twentieth-century houses, all with typical Arts and Crafts motifs. The features include decorative half-timbering, carved bargeboards, deep eaves, with rusticated stucco and feature stonework in a number of styles fashionable at the time. Richard Norman Shaw's Queen Anne style is replicated at Number Four and there is a Charles Voysey-influenced stucco example at Number Eighteen, with more obvious medieval detailing in many others. Brairdene is a mirror image of The Coign in plan, but with the omission of the central first-floor balcony and the attached 'motor house'.

The Coign is a brick-built, part-rendered, detached villa under a tiled gable roof. Built on a corner plot it has an L-shaped plan with two façades, which are divided by the large first-

Location: The Midlands

Date: 1912

Type: Arts and Crafts-influenced suburban villa (unlisted)

floor balcony with overhanging eaves and a porchway below. There is an original central chimney stack and an additional lateral one, added to accommodate recent internal changes in the rooms below. The gable end projects slightly, giving a hint of a medieval jetty, with a bay window tucked underneath and

THE COIGN

it is finished off by a diamond brick motif below the eaves. All the windows are casement with small leaded lights set into heavy timber mullions and, like all the architectural details in the house, indicate a heavy Arts and Crafts influence. Once inside, this influence prevails in the staircase and main fireplace and the more Victorian features such as terracotta-tiled floors and simple cornices, which blend in easily with the general aura of Arts and Crafts.

History

This avenue of houses was built in two periods straddling the First World War on arable land owned by Sir Richard Paget. Sir Richard imposed a restrictive covenant on any development of the land, including the number of houses that could be built and the quality of property allowed, which was reflected in the cost of each house (detached houses £380 and semis £360). The land was bought by a developer, M.A. Boswell Ltd, in 1911 and designs for some of the houses were submitted soon after by the architect E.J. Hartill. Most of the houses were built between 1912 and 1914. A gap occurred because of the Great War and building started again in 1918 and was completed by 1924. The size and quality of the properties indicates the type of owners who would originally have bought these houses, though whether this was a speculative development or if owners bought plots before building began is as yet undiscovered. One of the first occupiers appears to have been the daughter of Mr Boswell, a great advertisement for his properties. Although the houses were not large the plan allowed for domestic staff, as can be seen on the original bell board at The Coign, which indicates that one live-in servant was employed, and that three further bedrooms were available for the family.

The Coign has two distinct façades joined by the balcony and porchway in the angle of the L-shaped plan and is hidden by mature trees for much of the year. The windows appear to be randomly positioned and include a small triangular-shaped attic window and a ground-floor oval example.

The top section of the front door is glazed with square leaded lights, while below a series of narrow raised and studded panels offer a sense of the medieval. This feature is replicated on the doors to the motor house.

The brick fireplace, though not in its original central position, is built of thin Tudor-like bricks and features a Gothic arch, typical of the period.

The staircase is a wonderful lattice of heavy timbers with fixing pegs protruding from the joints in the medieval tradition, which rises from a hallway of terracotta floor tiles.

5. ARCHITECTURAL DETAILS

Architectural details can be found on the exterior and interior of a building. They may be contemporary with the structure or later additions. These features can be as important historically as the structure itself and it is useful to understand what styles and materials identify a particular building period. Many of the materials used for details have been already been discussed in Chapter Three as they are also used structurally, with the exception of metal. Some are attached to the building as additions such as downpipes, while others are integral to the house as in carved structural timbers, doors and windows. These features can be divided into two categories: those that are purely decorative, such as the ornamentation on a plaster ceiling; and functional items that have been embellished to improve their appearance, such as rainwater hoppers. The period façade is strongly affected by external features, changes in the type and positioning of such items as windows and doors can ruin the appearance of the house. Naturally, alterations to period houses have occurred in past centuries and are now seen as part of its history, but any future changes need to be considered carefully and will not necessarily be sanctioned for a listed property.

Windows and Glass

The size of early windows (or 'windholes', which is a likely origin of the word) was a compromise between letting light in and smoke from the fire out, while keeping out the harsher elements. Shutters regulated light and wind and even when windows became glazed, external shutters were often still present. Until glass was available or could be afforded oilcloth, waxed paper and horn were among the common alternatives, and the earliest inserts were attached on to a separate frame, so that the windows could be removed when the owners moved on. In 1579 a law was passed to stop owners taking windows away when they moved or from bequeathing them to someone in their will. Glass first appeared in large houses in the thirteenth century and by the beginning of sixteenth century it was more widely used, although some very basic dwellings did not have glass until the Georgian period. Early wooden framed windows probably developed from internal shutters and were often fitted between existing wooden or stone mullions. In wealthier homes, wrought-iron casements with glass were used; at first these did not open, although sometimes they had a pierced lead pane or one hinged section to allow air into the house, as at Eyam Hall in Derbyshire.

Period windows have two types of opening systems, casement and sash, and there are a number of shapes of windows and particular periods in history associated with their use. Casement windows are the earliest form and are hinged at the side, while sashes slide on runners, usually aided by a supporting mechanism. Many windows are fitted parallel to the wall, but projecting versions in the form of bay and oriel windows, often splayed to capture more light, were built in grand houses from the fifteenth century. Bay windows, either ground-floor versions or double height, are angular projections. The rounded versions are usually termed bows, as at the Elizabethan Burton Agnes Hall in Yorkshire of the seventeenth century, and were popular again in the Regency period. Oriel windows usually project from the upper storey and wooden versions require extra support in the form of corbels or brackets. Brick and stone examples are integral to the structure as at Rye House Gatehouse, East Sussex (circa 1443). Another early form of window was the dormer; the word,

Ramsgate, East Sussex (Grade II) A semi-detached villa, circa 1840, as part of J.C. Eddell's development of Vale Square, with the later addition of Art Nouveau stained glass to the window and door.

Lavenham, Suffolk (Grade II) This sixteenth-century timber-framed and plastered house shows three stages of window development: top left is a four-light wooden mullioned example; top right is an opening leaded casement; and below left is a Georgian sash.

flat sheet of glass. Small quarries (as panes were originally called) were cut, often in a diamond pattern, joined by strips of lead (called cames), then fixed between the lights (the spaces between the mullions). Leaded lights came in various forms and Walter Geede's book *100 Designs for Glaziers*, published in 1613, offered a wealth of inspiration to the seventeenth-century house builder. Designs of this period were revived in Tudoresque cottages of the nineteenth and twentieth centuries.

Although the sash window is synonymous with the Georgians, an early, less sophisticated sash is known to have been made in 1519. However, they were properly introduced for use around the 1670s and had eventually taken over from casements as standard windows in all but the poorest homes by the eighteenth century. Many casements were replaced with sashes during the eighteenth-century rebuilding period, despite the window tax and the levy on glass. The window tax, imposed in 1696, had some effect on the updating of houses, and, as a levy was paid if the house had more than six windows, many houses did block out windows (defenestrate) to avoid paying. It is likely that by the time that the tax was repealed in 1851 most of these would have been reopened, and that existing examples of blocked-up windows are

deriving from the Latin to sleep, supports a connection with the medieval period. As small apertures projecting from roofs, dormers were common in the sixteenth and seventeenth centuries, when hall houses were adapted to create an upper floor and light and air were needed in the new rooms.

Fully glazed opening windows were becoming more common by the sixteenth century, using glass called cylinder or broad sheet. By blowing and manipulating molten glass a cylinder could be made and by cutting off the ends, then slitting and opening the cylinder, this produced a large

Bibury, Gloucestershire (Grade II) A gable-ended dormer window (left) and a hipped dormer window (right); both are additions to this converted row of cottages.

Ludlow, Shropshire (Grade II) *This early seventeenth-century shop and house has two eighteenth-century bow-shaped oriel windows on the first floor, with lead roofs and plastered underhangs.*

Weobley Herefordshire (Grade II) Small diamond- and lozenge-shaped panes of glass make up this early sixteenth-century window, with one opening casement.

more likely to be a result of internal changes to rooms or part of the balancing of a classical façade (*see* Mayburys Case Study in Chapter Two). Some of the most visually interesting house fronts have been created by the insertion of sash windows into an earlier building that does not have the classical proportions to take them. Reduced-sized sashes, raised rooflines and a mixture of sash and casement are all solutions arrived at by the eighteenth-century fashion-conscious house owner.

Early examples of the sash window only opened at the bottom and were flush with the outside of the wall, as were all standard windows in the seventeenth century. When open, these early versions were held up by pegs, as can be seen at Arkwright's cottages in Cromford (1780), but these were superseded by the invention of the pulley and weight system with sash cords. There is some debate as to the exact origins of the sash window; it was possibly a Dutch-inspired idea, but it is now known across

Farnham, Surrey (Grade II) A horizontal Yorkshire sash in a row of workers' cottages of 1840.

the world as a quintessentially English product. An alternative for smaller houses, or for the smaller upper-storey windows, was the Yorkshire sash, a side-opening version running on a waxed wooden bead, first used in Yorkshire in the eighteenth century, as in the estate houses at Settrington, but soon made all over the country.

After the 1709 London Building Act, houses in the capital were required to build their windows a brick width of about 4in (100mm) back from the façade and later for the frame to be hidden behind the brickwork. These stipulations were not immediately put into practice elsewhere in the country and therefore dating a house on these factors alone is only accurate in London. Although sash windows usually required a larger aperture in the face of the house, the panes of glass were still quite small due to limitations of technique and cost. Small panes were secured by 'astragals' or glazing bars, which initially were made quite thick, some as much as 2in (50mm) wide, and made of hardwood, usually of unpainted oak. The painting of frames with white lead only started when inferior woods began to be used in the eighteenth century. By the end of the century there was a fashion for dark colours and in the next century a revival for broken whites, which have since been replaced in many cases with the modern stark white.

The sash window owes much to the development of crown or spun glass in the late seventeenth century, which was an improvement on cylinder glass in both quality of transparency and the size of pane produced. After first blowing a bubble, the molten glass was then spun, creating a disc of glass up to and sometimes exceeding 5ft (1.5m) in diameter, which was then cut into panes. The central base or bullion, though usually discarded, was occasionally used in a small dwelling, but rarely in full view on a façade, and this wastage made crown glass expensive compared to cylinder. In the second half of the eighteenth century, as glass became affordable, more modest houses increased the size of their windows and glazing bars became thinner, contributing to the elegance epitomized in Georgian buildings. The use of hand-blown glass waned as industrial casting methods produced polished plate in the late eighteenth century and sheet glass about a century later. Sash windows were also used in shipbuilding, and the open stern gallery on HMS *Victory*, Horatio Nelson's flagship, was replaced with twenty-seven individual part-opening sashes with storm shutters at her refit, which was completed in 1803.

Steyning, West Sussex (Grade II) This sixteenth-century timber-framed house was refaced in brick in 1705 under a tile and Horsham slate roof. The height of the house required a compromise in the sash window proportions, making them almost square.

Ludlow, Shropshire (Grade II) The façade, added to an earlier house, is eighteenth century and is dominated by Venetian windows, the centre ones with gothic fenestration. Note the thickness of the glazing bars on the upper floors in comparison with the slimmer ground-floor versions.

In a truly Georgian house, windows were largest on the first floor, where the piano nobile reception rooms were situated and the exterior surrounds of these windows were often enriched with details such as pilasters and balconies. The fashion for classical detailing in the seventeenth and eighteenth centuries was indulged even in some small houses with decorative windows such as the Venetian, a 'tripartite' sash window (also called Palladian), which was often used to create a lighter entrance hall. By the 1820s glazing bars had been reduced to around ¼in (10mm) and were sometimes made of metal as opposed to wood. With the development of larger sheets of plate glass many multi-pane sash windows were replaced in the middle of the nineteenth century by two- or four-pane types, allowing more light into the house. However, this glass was heavier and so the original timberwork needed to be strengthened with 'horns' to take the extra weight of plate glass. A Georgian house with horns suggests that the windows are later, or that an alteration has been made to allow plate glass to be used.

Bow windows are synonymous with Regency seaside towns and shop fronts, but, generally, projecting windows did not become widespread until the repeal of the excise duty on glass in 1845, because of the large expanse of glass they required. By 1851, with taxes on glass and windows consigned to history, glass was promoted on a large scale with the designing of the Crystal Palace Exhibition Hall, which created a new

Ramsgate, Kent (Grade II) Spencer Square, built during the first half of the nineteenth century, has examples of thin glazing bars made from cast iron.

Emsworth, Hampshire (Grade II*) The large-paned windows of plate glass with supporting horns of sometime after the 1840s are additions to this Georgian house of 1780.

Lyme Regis, Dorset (Grade II) Double-height bow windows of 1815–19.

interest in home conservatories. Late Victorian and particularly Edwardian windows grew in

size as glass became cheaply produced in large panes; glazing bars all but disappeared and the sash window was reduced to two or four panes. Industrial mass-production made the use of

Odiham, Hampshire (Grade II) The façade of this seventeenth-century house has been substantially altered by the addition of bay windows in the Victorian period.

Derby, Derbyshire *The use of Venetian windows, as part of the Queen Anne Revival of the middle of the nineteenth century, is seen here with stained glass and decorative panelling.*

Birmingham, West Midlands (Grade II) *Jettying, imitation half-timbering, oriel and bay windows were all used in the development at Bournville at the beginning of the twentieth century, giving a sense of the medieval.*

decorative and coloured glass popular for many homes. Bay windows again became an important feature, this time in small by-law houses of the 1870s, and are best known during the mass building of Victorian and Edwardian terraced houses. Although casement windows had never entirely disappeared, there was a long time when they were seen as inappropriate for a fashionable house and many were replaced during the Georgian and Victorian periods. By the late nineteenth century, under the influence of the Arts and Crafts Movement, there was a revival in the wooden casement, which was one of the features of a good solid house of this period and continued into the mock Tudor houses of the 1920s and 30s.

Doors

The entrance has always been one of the most important social elements of a house, sometimes raised and including steps to further elevate its status. Doorways are often enhanced by pilasters or a portico, or at the very least some sort of projection above the door to protect visitors from the weather. These have developed from simple drip mouldings or overhangs to elaborate hoods and porchways. The building of wooden pillared porticoes only stopped when the building acts of the eighteenth century discouraged the use of combustible materials on façades. Other materials were used to decorate the exterior of the

Romsey, Hampshire (Grade II) *The entrance to this late eighteenth-century house has all the elements to lend it status: a commanding door, with a fanlight under a large portico, is reached by a substantial flight of steps.*

Lyme Regis, Dorset (Grade II) *Although Regency, this cast-iron trellised door canopy appears to be using sunburst and clouds, the later motifs of Art Deco.*

doorway. Stone was popular in areas where the material was indigenous or where small amounts could be afforded, and craftsmen, skilled in rubbed and carved brickwork, were in constant demand. By the late eighteenth century the decorative qualities of wrought and then cast iron began to be appreciated, producing porches and hoods and these continued to be fashionable throughout the next century.

During the eighteenth century the hall and staircase became the most important part of the house, requiring large amounts of natural light. Early 'overdoor lights' were rectangular but soon semicircular 'fanlights' (a name coined late in the eighteenth century) became fashionable

and the earliest fan-shaped over-door light is in a volume of *Vitruvius Britannicus*, published in 1725. Fanlights probably originated from the fashion for arched windows and the repeating of this design above the door, as can be seen at The Crescent in Shrewsbury (*see* Chapter Two). Sometimes this arched window was duplicated on an inner door, which was called the 'Dutch Plan'. Fanlights were initially associated with grand houses, but soon became widespread and can be found in some shape or form in many smaller houses. As part of fashionable updating, many fanlights were added to earlier doorcases. Fanlights are merely windows with a greater element of detailing. Early glazing bars were produced in wood and looked rather heavy.

simpler as fashions changed. Some examples feature a central circle with the house number painted in the middle, with the central circle sometimes opening for ventilation. Regency designs included such names as 'batswing' and 'teardrop'.

As the Victorian era began, the interest in fanlights disappeared in London and the south, although the fashion continued a little longer in areas further from the capital. The ground plans of many terraced houses did not give enough light to the hall, and in some cases there was inadequate ceiling height to add a fanlight. Glazing the top panels of the door became a popular alternative, and while this practice started in the Georgian period it is associated more with the Victorians. As large panes of glass were

Sandwich, Kent (Grade II) A later owner of this fifteenth-century timber-framed house was determined to update in the fashionable style and has squeezed in an overdoor light and hood along the angle of the original jetty. Dated 1756, it also marks the boundary between two parishes.

However, by the 1760s slimmer versions were available using a combination of wrought iron and lead and later cast lead. *The Practical Builder* by William Pain, published in 1774, in common with many architectural pattern books of the eighteenth century showed a massive range of designs for fanlights, and it was during this time that the most detailed and complicated designs were available using small panes of glass.

By the nineteenth century, further complexity was made possible by using large sheets of plate glass behind complex ironwork, which freed designers to make more detailed designs attached to one sheet of glass. However, despite these technical innovations some designs became

Southampton, Hampshire (Grade II) Within this early nineteenth-century door the glass panels are hinged to allow ventilation to the hallway.

Overdoor lights.

Overdoor lights, or the curved versions called fanlights, appear in a range of styles.

a) A fan-shaped design above a raised panel door.	*b) An eighteenth-century version, probably designed by a chairmaker.*	*c) Curvilinear tracery, a design sometimes containing a house number.*
d) A gothic example from John Wood (1768).	*e) A fanlight, complete with later stained-glass side lights.*	*f) The classic fan design.*

now available, doors in Victorian houses became heavily glazed, with coloured or frosted glass for privacy while the addition of side lights increased the natural light entering the hall.

The height of doorways has changed significantly over the past 500 years, due to the generally increased height of people and the fashion for higher ceilings. The widths of doors were variable, too, most likely determined in vernacular houses by the size of planks or the gap available between two supports, or, in fashionable houses, by the size of women's skirts. The door width became standardized during the Victorian era. Early doors did not have independent frames, but were hung straight on to one of the structural posts of timber-framed houses. Stone buildings used a pin (straight into wall) and

Lavenham, Suffolk *An early plank and ledge oak door, indicated by the horizontal rows of studs.*

strap (around door) hinge; the Jew's House in Lincoln is a twelfth-century example of this method. It was not until the sixteenth century that independent door frames were built and early L- and H-shaped hinges or more ornate versions are still found on many period doors. Early doors were made with the plank and ledge method sometimes with a diagonal brace, creating solid heavy versions. Initially made of oak, this eventually proved uneconomical and owners of small houses started using softwoods.

During the late sixteenth century a development produced the panelled door, which became standard in more modest houses from the eighteenth century. Much more reliant upon jointing methods, created from horizontal 'rails' and vertical 'stiles', the panelled door was a lighter product and became the final design solution for wooden doors. Over the period of the next 150 years a massive range of different designs for doors was produced. The number of panels altered from as few as two in the seventeenth-century examples to the standard six or eight panels found on most Georgian houses and these could be raised (fielded) or recessed. As the eighteenth century progressed, doors became more substantial again, probably as a result of the importation of cheap pine or deal, timber that was suitable to paint or grain. It was necessary to protect exterior softwood doors with paint; colours have ranged from dark green or brown in the Georgian period to green or black during most of Victoria's reign, with brighter colours appearing by the turn of the twentieth century.

Ceramic Details

Terracotta, the Latin for 'cooked earth', is a fine red or yellow earthenware clay that is known more as a sculptor's material than a builder's, but, with further refining, it is in fact a suitable material with which to produce ornate architectural detailing. It was first used in England in the sixteenth century to decorate the palaces and houses of the wealthy. Sutton Place in Surrey (1525–26) is an example of the early use of this material, followed by evidence of its use nearby

Sandwich, Kent (Grade II*) The original nine-panelled oak door from the seventeenth century appears to have been even shorter at one time.

Cranbrook, Kent (Grade II) An eighteenth-century two-panelled door inserted into this late fifteenth-century Wealden cloth hall.

at Henry VIII's lost palace of Nonsuch (1538). The invention of Coade Stone in the eighteenth century enabled more modest houses to be embellished with clay decoration. The Coade Artificial Stone Manufactory, initially in Lyme Regis, produced a pale, clay-based artificial stone from 1769 to 1840, which is often mistaken for the real thing. The soft material was pressed into plaster moulds, dried, then fired in the same way as clay and was used for architectural detailing and statuary. The London Building Acts, banning the use of wood for external details, created a large market for this material, and the company later moved to London under the leadership of Eleanor Coade, eventually becoming one of the first companies

to offer mail order to customers both at home and abroad. Many famous architects, such as Adams, Nash and Soane, came to rely on the material to produce details on façades, chimney-pieces and garden features, and examples can still be seen in many places, including Buckingham Palace and Bedford Square in London, and Sledmere House in Yorkshire.

A revival of true terracotta occurred in the following century, when Victorian architects took to the material for both external and internal detailing. Large commercial buildings, churches and museums were decorated with terracotta, as its cost was comparable to that of cheap stone and there also was a belief in its pollution-resistant properties. Harrods Department Store

Derby, Derbyshire Variations in door panels
continued throughout the 1920s and 1930s, like this
example added to a Victorian house.

Emsworth, Hampshire (Grade II) This early
nineteenth-century house has small additions of
Coade Stone attached to the brick façade.

*Great Exhibition Catalogue
(1851)* Tudor-style terracotta
chimneys by Doulton & Co
were featured at the
exhibition.

in London (completed in 1905) has an exterior
of Doulton's yellow terracotta with some excellent interior detailing, while the Natural History
Museum (1873–81) by Alfred Waterhouse, also
in London, is polychromatic architecture at its
best. Victorian taste was excited by both the
range of colours and the delicate detailing produced from terracotta and it became a firm
favourite for middle-class homes. Porch and hall
floors were covered in encaustic tiles, originally
produced by Mintons in 1840, the colour of

which was inlaid in the medieval tradition, rather than painted. The enormous demand for factory-made detailing for both the inside and outside of buildings led to quality-control problems, with the result that within a decade into the new century, terracotta and the level of ornamentation it produced had lost its appeal.

Metal detailing

Wrought iron has been used for practical elements of the house since the medieval period, for example the Suffolk latch, early boot scrapers, doorknockers and hinges. As in much early decoration, designs of the seventeenth century were based on nature, and it was only with the introduction of cast iron in the eighteenth century that more complicated representations became possible. Patterns that had been popular for wrought iron were copied in the new material, although cast iron did not take over entirely as there were parts of railings and balconies that required the greater strength offered by wrought iron. The process of casting iron, mass-produced in foundries rather than at the blacksmith's forge, made iron much more economical to use, and with the building boom of the late eighteenth and early nineteenth centuries metal detailing on buildings became widespread. Cast iron was initially associated with industrial buildings, but it was given a royal seal of approval when it was used in the construction of the Brighton Pavilion for the Prince Regent in 1821. The Regency period used a wide range of influences from abroad, which was expressed through its balconies, verandas and porches in places such as Leamington Spa and Cheltenham, and the seaside resorts of Sussex and Kent.

Melbourne, Derbyshire (Grade I) The famous ironworker Robert Bakewell of Derby made this lyre-patterned wrought-iron balustrade in 1725. (By kind permission of Melbourne House)

Ramsgate, Kent (Grade II) *Number Eight, The Paragon, built around 1816, makes the most of the Regency love of decorative ironwork.*

As the industrial age progressed it brought greater expertise in the use of metal, while the dissemination of style books and other forms of design influence promoted a whole range of items, including staircases and garden furniture. In 1823, Lewis Nockalls Cottingham published his pattern book, *The Ornamental Metal Worker's Directory*, which was to prove influential across the world. There was also a proliferation of designs on offer from well-established foundries such as The Coalbrookdale Company and the Carron Company, whose pattern books and company catalogues were full of designs for embellishing the exterior of a house, including, by the middle of the eighteenth century, fanlights. For the speculative builder it was cheaper to have the same design cast for a whole development of houses, so a change in ironwork design on terraces tends to indicate sections that were built at different times. External ironwork in both Georgian and Regency architecture was usually painted grey and occasionally blue or green. There is a common misconception that black was the traditional colour for railings, but this was a Victorian practice.

Letter boxes (first known as letter plates) and house numbers arrived with the advent of the national postal system in the nineteenth century, when it became important to identify individual houses with greater accuracy. Door furniture became very ornate and was available in brass, which is a Victorian tradition and not indicative of the Georgian period as is often thought. In this period of elaborate decoration roofs did not escape decorative detailing, and the ornamental cresting on a roof called brattishing was a popular Victorian addition made from metal or terracotta. Original metal detailing may be identifiable, as it was the practice of many foundries to sign and date their pieces. However, the wholesale destruction of metal items such as railings for the war effort in 1940 means that many seen today are replacements.

Rainwater goods were produced as much to collect rainwater as they were to protect the fabric of the building. The Dissolution of the Monasteries was the catalyst for an upsurge in lead work using second-hand material, which created many attractive hopper heads and cisterns. These were cast in lead and decorated, and it was not until the early eighteenth century that cast iron and zinc were adopted for the making of these items. The fashion for parapet walls allowed gutters to be hidden and a lead box gutter was built behind the parapet to collect the rain. Downpipes were more difficult to hide, but some Georgian builders used a recessed downpipe, let into the brickwork and the rest were painted to reduce their impact. Cast iron enabled some innovation to take place in drainage, as in the structural columns on the Crystal Palace, which doubled as downpipes. Some architects

Portsmouth, Hampshire *A beautifully preserved pair of Victorian terrace houses with cast iron and stained glass detailing.*

went to great lengths to reduce the visual impact of rainwater goods, including hiding the gutters within the bottom rows of roofing slates, as was undertaken by Edwin Lutyens. Badly placed gutters and downpipes, often painted to stand out from the wall colour, can be visual eyesores on a period house; where they are not original to the fabric of the building their impact should be minimized.

Internal Features

Materials used inside the house were, in many cases, the same as the external ones, but interior detailing was often more elaborate, as it was protected from the weather. Decoration echoes the influences of the time and particular motifs can be found expressed in each period. Tudor roses are an obvious example of the sixteenth century and acanthus leaves, a classical influence, of the seventeenth and eighteenth centuries. However, revivals in the use of patterns and motifs can be confusing when trying to date details, particularly when they may be only a few decades apart. Most timber items were treated in some decorative fashion, as in the chamfering of ceiling beams and the carving of stair newels and balusters. It was only later, when early period houses were remodelled, that other materials like ornate plaster and metal were used decoratively.

Staircases

The first proper staircases were made from stone and found in large houses and churches, and

Abinger, Surrey (Grade II*) Like so many Arts and Crafts architects, Edwin Lutyens designed many interior details in his houses, such as this door furniture at Goddards. (By kind permission of the Landmark Trust)

Singleton, West Sussex Re-creation of an early staircase leading to the solar above. (By kind permission of The Weald & Downland Open Air Museum)

Titchfield, Hampshire (Grade II) A typical layout of a staircase winding around the central chimney stack in this timber-framed house of the middle of the seventeenth century.

therefore it was masons, not joiners, who first invented the staircase. Early stairs often wound around a stone newel in a spiral built within a turret, or in the thickness of an outside wall. Defensible bastel houses in the north had living quarters upstairs serviced by a straight stone flight on the outside. In early small timber houses, where there was an upper storey, it was accessed by a simple wooden ladder. By the sixteenth century, as carpenters reproduced the work of the stonemasons in construction and design, ladders evolved into staircases made from blocks of timber (often quartered oak trunks). Newel stairs were constructed around a vertical post, and this method was used until the

eighteenth century and even the early nineteenth century for modest houses in some areas. As soon as chimney stacks were common in small houses, the natural place for the staircase was tucked around the stack in short flights. Where stairs were inserted into an older house, they needed to be relatively small, to fit into the existing structure and preserve the constructional integrity, but when many of these houses were rebuilt in brick or stone, it was time to emulate the grand staircases of the wealthy. In slightly larger houses, with no space restrictions, the straight flight of stairs was commonly used, and the dog-leg appeared from the late sixteenth century, becoming quite common a century later

Bramber, West Sussex (Grade I) An ornate seventeenth-century closed string staircase with a cherub decorating the newel post. (By kind permission of St Mary's)

(*see* the Luntley Court Case Study in Chapter Three). Early staircases were closed string, having a continuous side panel of oak and with carved, if rather chunky, handrails and flat balusters with newel posts. In smaller houses staircases were built with closed strings until the eighteenth century, as they were cheaper and easier to construct.

Open well stairs appeared from mid seventeenth century, using a greater allowance of space, with the result that the staircase began to be a prominent feature (*see* New Place Case Study in Chapter Five). As in many situations, the fashion for staircases in smaller houses mirrored those first appearing in grand regional

houses, and by the seventeenth century three basic designs for the staircase had evolved: the well; the dog-leg; and the newel (or winder).

By the end of the century the chimney stack was built on an end wall to create space for an impressive reception hall, with gently sweeping stairs rising to the first-floor piano nobile rooms. From thereon, the higher up the house the stairs went, the simpler they became, past the bedrooms to the servants' quarters. Houses did not have to be very large before a second staircase for the servants was desirable, and this was often in the form of a tight, narrow newel or dog-leg with little or no architectural detailing. As carpentry techniques improved through the

Southampton, Hampshire (Grade II) An open string staircase with decorated stair ends and simple stick balusters (circa 1835).

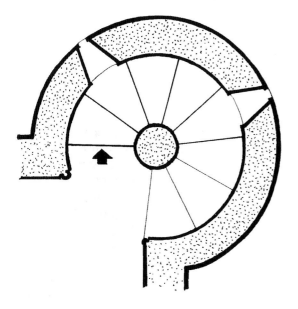

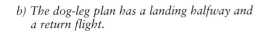

a) The winder (or newel) generally turns to the right around a central vertical support and has steep risers.

b) The dog-leg plan has a landing halfway and a return flight.

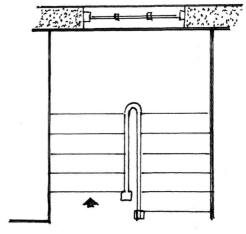

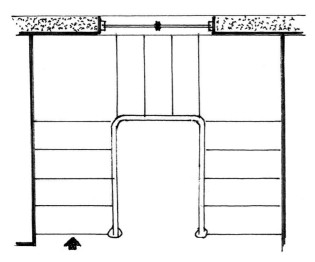

c) The well stair has a central void and is the most spacious of the three types.

Staircases.

Lavant, Sussex This Arts and Crafts house, built in 1912, reverts back to early influences in its use of oak and closed string stairs.

eighteenth century, staircases became lighter in build with slimmer, simpler balusters giving a sense of space to the main architectural feature. The main change in the late eighteenth century was the use of the open string staircase (sometimes cantilevered), a more expensive method with the stair ends exposed and decorated, therefore found first in larger houses, but with all but very basic houses soon following the fashion.

After 1721, when importation costs from the British West Indies were lifted by The Naval Stores Act, mahogany became affordable and its use in banister rails contrasted well with painted softwood uprights. This, and the beginning of the use of cast iron, meant that many more house owners could afford elegant and detailed

stairs (*see* the Eaton Lodge Case Study in Chapter Five). The fashion for ornate metal balusters continued throughout the Regency and Victorian periods, with staircases only simplifying in design during the Edwardian period. The return to medieval styles during the late nineteenth century under the influence of the Arts and Crafts Movement led to a revival in simple staircases. This simplicity continued through the 1920s and the International Style of the 1930s, but although the latter appeared to be avantgarde, there is a sense of the medieval in the use of the curved staircase or half-circular stair turret.

Titchfield, Hampshire Titchfield Abbey, housing a Carthusian order of monks in the thirteenth century, became a house shortly after 1537, at which point home comforts such as fireplaces were added. (By kind permission of English Heritage)

Branscombe, Devon (Grade II*) This house was once the parlour wing of a larger dwelling and contains restored plank and muntin panelling and elaborately carved ceiling timbers, but a surprisingly plain fireplace. (© Ian Sumner; reproduced by kind permission of the Landmark Trust)

Fireplaces

Until the wholesale introduction of central heating in the twentieth century the fireplace was the most important functional element inside the house. Initially in the middle of the room, the open fire was moved to one end and a 'smoke hood' made from wood and plaster inserted. From the sixteenth century, chimney stacks of stone or brick became common, as these materials were incombustible and more robust. A surround to frame the hearth opening was required and during the sixteenth century, in the stone houses of the wealthy, these were embellished with detailed carving on the lintel. However, in smaller dwellings these lintels usually remained plain. In timber-framed houses the bressumer, a large baulk of timber, was used to support the stack; in smaller houses it tended to be left undecorated. These early hearths had firedogs to support large logs and to contain the fire. By the eighteenth century, wrought-iron baskets were used, the precursor to Georgian register grates.

By the seventeenth century, the whole section of the chimney inside the room was decorated and referred to as a chimney-piece. These became highly ornate and, as in all detailing, the extent and the quality of the carving indicated

Bromfield, Shropshire (Grade II*) This chimney-piece was built from an assortment of Jacobean carving brought from elsewhere. (© Paul Barker; reproduced by kind permission of the Landmark Trust)

the status of the household. The general design of chimney-pieces simplified as classical influences were adopted, finally consisting of a projecting shelf or lintel with supporting verticals, giving the fire a surround with attached mantelpiece which has changed little since the eighteenth century. What did alter was the size of the aperture and the quantity and quality of detailing attached to the overall shape. By the eighteenth century, three-dimensional classical details such as columns, fluted pilasters, swags and pediments were typically made in marble, stone or wood.

By the late Georgian period how to produce an efficient fire was known and the opening of the fireplace became smaller, finally concentrating the fire into fitted grates made of either cast iron or polished steel, which revolutionized the look of the fireplace. Fire surrounds were influenced by fashionable styles such as the Gothic revival. By the middle of the nineteenth century a typical fire surround, while very simple, had lost the delicate qualities of the Georgian period and taken on a chunky appearance. Contrasting with this simplicity the metal grates became very detailed, as the techniques of the industrial age

Eyam, Derbyshire (Grade II) A Georgian fireplace and grate were added to Eyam Hall, a seventeenth-century house.

and the affordability of mass-production were realized. Tiles decorating the splayed sides of the opening were popular and included English imitations of Dutch 'Delft tiles'. Later designs were influenced by the English Aesthetic, the Arts and Crafts Movement and European Art Nouveau. Fireplaces of the 1920s and 1930s began to be supplemented with electric fires, and the gradual move towards the installation of central heating in the average home meant the end of the reliance on the open fire.

Floors and Ceilings

Early floors in modest homes were made from rammed clay or earth and there is evidence of a number of other materials that were mixed in to give a more hard-wearing surface. There are regional differences. For example, in the East Midlands, there was a tradition of plaster floors. In the slightly better homes of the seventeenth and eighteenth centuries the ground floors were of stone flags or brick, with marble and an early form of wood block being used in prestigious houses. Suspended timber floors in living areas were not introduced for small houses until the eighteenth century, and consisted of wide boards

Wolverhampton, West Midlands This mass-produced bedroom fireplace is contemporary to the house built in 1912.

of oak, elm or deal, varying considerably in size. The plank width reduced during the Georgian period, and, as softwoods became common, floorboards were stained and stencilled.

Derby, Derbyshire (Grade I) The flagstone entrance of Pickfords House (1770).

By the nineteenth century, timber was the usual material for floors in new houses and was machine-cut to a standard width, but it was not made into a feature as it was commonly covered by carpet and later linoleum. There was renewed interest in a hardwood block flooring called parquet (first popular in the palaces of France), and for ground-floor hallways terracotta tiles were indicative of Victorian style.

As soon as houses had upper floors there was an opportunity to decorate the underside of the timber joists and many were lime washed to lighten the downstairs rooms. Ceiling timbers were treated in a number of ways, from detailed carving to the more common chamfering and stops. Exposed timber ceilings re-occurred in the late nineteenth century, as part of the medieval revival. Early exposed joists without any form of

Portsmouth, Hampshire *Matching terracotta tiles on the floors of the porch and conservatory were put in when the house was built in 1862–63 (see the Eaton Lodge Case Study in Chapter Five).*

fashioning tend to indicate a service area rather than the main living spaces. All the ceilings in small medieval houses would have had exposed timbers until plaster became available and a new ceiling could be afforded. Decoratively painted ceiling timbers are rare in English houses, but are often found in Scotland, such as the stunning seventeenth-century ceiling at Gladstone's Land in Edinburgh.

During the sixteenth century, plaster became the standard way to cover and soundproof a ceiling in all but the most basic houses, and so ceiling timbers were left rough because they were to be plastered over. Rough timbers, which were not designed to be exposed but which have been uncovered subsequently, can be identified by the rough markings of keying tools or regular holes from nails used to attach laths prior to plastering. From the sixteenth century onwards, simple plaster ceilings painted white are common in quite modest houses and more decorative versions are found from the eighteenth century. Central ceiling roses were first used in the eighteenth century, but, like the decorated corbels that project from a wall to support an arch or beam, are recognizable parts of a Victorian interior. Ceilings made of papier-mâché were introduced in the eighteenth century in larger houses,

Wolverhampton, West Midlands *In some parts of the country terracotta continued to be popular well into the twentieth century, representing a time lag in architectural fashion as in this example of just before the First World War.*

Lavant, West Sussex *This is a beautiful example of the medieval influences apparent in Arts and Crafts architecture. Heavy oak beams and reclaimed black and white tiles feature in this example designed in 1912 by Edward S. Prior.*

a) Eyam Hall (1676).	b) Pickfords House (1770).
c) The Regency Town House, Hove (1825).	

Known details like cornices that can be visited will assist in the dating of your own features.

as in the drawing rooms at The Vyne in Hampshire (circa 1760). Layers of paper were pasted together and dried, the result being a very strong material that could even be used to build furniture. Like all new trends, it eventually became affordable as a ceiling decoration for

Southampton, Hampshire (Grade II) A cornice (circa 1835) showing flowers with a classical pattern below is just one of several elaborate cornices in this late Georgian terrace.

Chawton, Hampshire (Grade II) Sixteenth-century wall paintings depicting heraldic motifs and hunting scenes.

smaller houses, and by the following century preformed decoration was being produced by a number of firms in the Midlands.

For centuries, the blurring of the angle between walls and ceiling has been a common practice. The frieze at the top of the wall began this, and during the Georgian period very detailed plaster cornices carried the tradition into the next century. Cornices are usually made of plaster, although they may be of wood, stone or papier-mâché, like so much of the detailing of this period. The designs for Georgian examples are based on the classical orders, but, as the Regency period arrived, cornices became influenced by a variety of cultures. In 1856 a patent was granted to produce fibrous moulding, the plaster being reinforced by canvas, making the process of making and fixing cornices much easier.

Walls

The majority of wall painting is medieval and mainly found in ecclesiastical buildings, where it has often been hidden for centuries behind the iconoclastic whitewash of the Reformation. Typical colours used, along with black and white, were earth-based dark reds and yellows,

with the occasional use of the more expensive blues and greens. Early inns also have some good examples, as in the Flushing Inn at Rye in East Sussex, in which a colourful painting of around 1537 depicts animals, birds and flowers, including a Tudor rose. The discovery of wall paintings in homes is rare because of the delicacy of the materials and the transient nature of fashionable detailing, but examples do exist, such as the early example at South Elmham Hall, Norfolk (circa 1270).

Dartington, Devon (Grade II) Eighteenth-century wall painting, one of several found in this thatched cottage; translated from the Latin as meaning 'peace within'.

It is likely that many painted plaster walls were hidden behind later panelling or painted over when houses changed hands. For damp and draughty medieval homes, panelling, as a method of finishing interior walls, was the perfect solution. Covering internal walls with wood was well established by the medieval period, and may have been a development of the wooden partitioning found in early hall and cross-passage houses. In modest period houses early panels were either of the plank and muntin type or small, square and plain, covering the whole wall using oak where available in a cross-hatch of stiles and rails. Panelling was at its most popular during the Tudor and Jacobean periods. Often limewashed, it functioned as a barrier to moisture and draughts, was hard-wearing and demonstrated the status of the owner by the amount of detail and carving afforded. By the seventeenth century, hardwoods (other than oak) and later imported softwoods were being used, and the panels had changed to reflect simpler classical proportions. The cheaper softwoods were not suitable to be left untreated, and so panels were painted, gilded, wood-grained and marbled. By the early eighteenth century, panelling had been reduced to below the dado rail in polite architecture. Half-panelling became

standard by the middle of the century and allowed the use of expensive wallpaper or damask fabric to be attached above, where it was less likely to be damaged. In smaller houses, half-panelling often took the form of vertical planks but this vernacular version has more to do with insulation and protecting the wall than following fashion.

With the total demise of panelling in the late eighteenth century, the base of the plaster wall needed to be protected with a skirting board. Made usually of wood in smaller houses, the height and detail varied considerably, although all period boards are typically tall with a chamfered or more ornate top. Walls were still divided up according to classical proportions through the Regency period, and largely continued throughout the Victorian and Edwardian periods, but with the addition of a picture rail. A resurgence in panelling came during the Victorian period, with an interest in dark woods to match the gloomy colours of the period. Panelling continued to be fashionable during the medieval revival brought about by the Arts and Crafts movement and continued into the twentieth century.

Internal shuttering, also a medieval solution to improve a draughty house, is now seen more

Bramber, West Sussex (Grade I) These wall panels were painted in the late sixteenth century and are an early example of trompe l'œil. Through the arched windows there are views of land and seascapes. (By kind permission of St Mary's)

Bath, Somerset (Grade I) The interior Georgian panelling of this house of 1720 has been restored and painted in an appropriate finish. (© Ian Sumner; reproduced by kind permission of the Landmark Trust)

as a feature of the eighteenth and nineteenth centuries. Georgian shutters were sectional and folded back into boxes at the side of the window or were raised on pulleys from below. The number of sections to a shutter depended on the size of the window, and this in turn was dictated (for houses built after the 1774 Building Act) by the 'rate' attributed to the house. Like all detailing, the quality of decoration on each panel is indicative of the status of the owner, although it may also reflect the age of the house, as early Georgian shutters tended to be simpler, complementing the rest of the interior scheme. The Victorian period introduced technology in the form of a rolling shutter operated with sash cords, but by the turn of the century the fashion for shutters had disappeared, due perhaps to the improved heating in large houses and the cost of craftsmanship.

Wallpaper

European wallpaper dates from the sixteenth century and was used on walls and ceilings; it was initially an expensive commodity, as it was hand-coloured over the basic block print. It did not entirely take the place of painting and stencilling on plaster, but it had the advantage of

Hove, East Sussex (Grade I) The houses on Brunswick Square were designed with this space-saving version of window shutters that rise vertically and therefore do not require deep window recesses to house them. Below them is an example of ornate panelling of the Regency period (see Brunswick Square Case Study in Chapter Six).

not being permanently fixed to the wall. The paper was attached to canvas on a wooden frame, which was tacked on to the plaster, the air gap between protecting the paper from the high levels of moisture found in many walls. By the seventeenth century, England was leading the way in wallpaper technology. Designs were block-printed or stencilled on to small single sheets and by the end of the century, the sheets were being joined up to produce rolls and were printed with multiple colours. This form of decoration seems to have appealed to the upwardly mobile 'merchant community', and would have eventually been a cheaper alternative to tapestry for the more modest household. Papers were inspired by textiles and tapestries, many imported by the East India Company, and

papers imitating drapery, panelling and marble started the fascination for the deceptive art of 'trompe l'œil'. A greater choice of colours and patterns became available as the technique of printing overlays of several colours was mastered, which reduced the need to hand-colour. This paved the way for the industrial methods early the following century. Flocking was especially popular throughout the eighteenth and nineteenth centuries, clearly intended to imitate cloth, as particles of wool were sprinkled over designs that had been block-printed with glue. At certain times there was encouragement to use particular colours; for example, in the first half of the eighteenth century blue was promoted in an attempt to protect the indigo dyeing trade.

A wallpaper tax was introduced in 1712, and all papers had to be stamped to confirm that the duty had been paid. At first, the stamp consisted of the Stuart arms of Queen Anne, but, from 1714 on the accession of George I, this changed to the initials GR intertwined with a crown and code letters and later GRIII, until the tax was abolished for British-made papers in 1836. The nineteenth century saw the mechanization of the printing methods and continuous rolls of wallpaper were produced from the 1830s. Wallpaper for smaller houses was the expanding market and was catered for by papers made in factories powered by steam, which speeded up manufacturing and reduced prices. Numerous pattern books showed a wide range of wallpapers. These were often a poorly designed eclectic mixture of influences dictated by production methods, as could be seen in the over-fussy designs at the 1851 Great Exhibition. Victorian wallpapers were dominated by the floral and the embossed, of which Anaglypta and Lincrusta are most common. As single-colour papers, they were used below the dado rail in conjunction with a more detailed paper above.

Not until the middle of the nineteenth century was there an attempt to improve the design of papers through such influences as the *Grammar of Ornament* by Owen Jones (1856). However, it was the leading designers and architects of the

Titchfield, Hampshire (Grade II) This mid eighteenth-century wallpaper, found in a loft space, comes complete with its date stamp and seems to imitate plasterwork of the period.

Arts and Crafts Movement who took basic design concepts and produced collections of well-considered wallpapers. William Morris produced around seventy designs for wallpapers and fabrics between 1864 and 1896, and, although in many cases these were hand-printed and therefore too expensive for the masses, his influence was widespread and has had a profound and sustained effect on the designing of flat pattern.

What we consider to be permanent fixtures in a house have, in the past, been considered as transitory, to be taken when the owners moved houses. Early windows, wooden floorboards, panelling and wallpaper attached to frames were all regarded as the sort of expensive items that could be taken away or assigned to another in a will. Only recently has it become inappropriate to strip a house of its features before leaving and to recognize the relevance of period features retained in their designed space as important reflections of the era.

The Great Exhibition (1851) This page shows the fussiness of industrially manufactured wallpaper of the time.

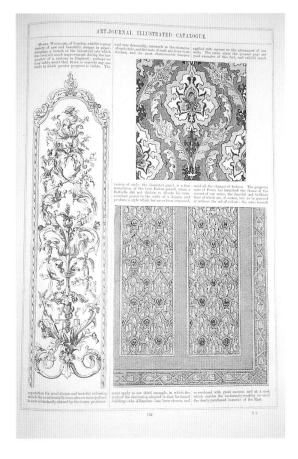

Description

Eaton Lodge is one of a pair of detached villas, with walls of stock brick built in a stretcher bond with stone quoins at the corners. There is evidence of archetypal Victorian architectural decoration, including heavy dripstones outlining the first-floor windows and brattishing on the ridge of the red tiled roof. Originally, the flat façade with its ground-floor bay and projecting porch (still apparent on its twin, Wellesley Villa) would have been covered in stucco, but sometime later the ground-floor wall was projected forward by several feet and the brick left bare. From the Ordnance Survey map of 1887 and the knowledge that the house was rented until 1895 and therefore not likely to have been substantially altered, it can be surmised that the alteration of the façade took place at the turn of the century. The extension creates larger ground-floor rooms with a veranda above, but

Location: Hampshire

Date: 1862–63

Type: Victorian detached (unlisted)

the detailing to the new façade is heavy, with pilastered bay windows and a pierced parapet wall to the roof terrace. The house retains wonderful original terracotta floors in the porchway and conservatory (*see* Chapter Five). The simple ground-floor bay window with a hipped roof to the east side of the house, an incongruous

EATON LODGE

later addition, appears to be more Arts and Crafts than Victorian and seems to be out of place with the rest of the house.

History

The deeds to this house state that in 1861 a widow, Rebecca Samways, with the help of her brother Daniel West, a builder, purchased land for £220, with a private mortgage from a well-known local jeweller, Emanuel Emanuel. They borrowed a further £500 to build on what had been arable land belonging to the architect Thomas Ellis Owen, who developed much of this part of Portsea Island. The plot was large enough for two detached houses with gardens and the necessary outbuildings, including a conservatory and was a stone's throw from the sea on one side and the East Hampshire Cricket Ground on the other. Rate books identify Daniel as the owner as, at that time, it was not seemly for women to own property. When Rebecca married the Rev. Mr Cooke in 1863, her new husband had a document drawn up allowing the income from the properties left to her by her first husband and her newly built ones to be retained by her rather than by himself, as the law at that time required. Eaton Lodge was built to be leased for the income and a number of tenants lived in the house over the next thirty years, including Mrs Wilmot Ellis, a widow with six children and two servants listed in the census in 1881. In 1895 Rebecca Cooke sold Eaton Place for £800 to Frederick Sydney Rouse and it is likely that it was at this time that the addition to the façade took place. In 1925 it changed hands again to a local solicitor George Bramsdon Addison and it has had five owners since that time.

The front entrance is a good example of the influence of Gothic architecture on Victorian design. The doorway has a heavy stone surround with a Gothic arch above the overdoor light and acanthus leaf balls at each side framing the door.

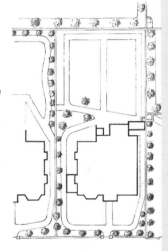

This measured drawing from the Ordnance Survey maps of 1865 and 1887 shows the plan of the house and layout of the garden. The house has one front bay and a projecting porch, the main part being a mirror image of the house next door.

The original wood and cast-iron staircase features unusual carved wooden knots, called 'Monkeys Fists', on the top of each newel post. This was a knot to weight the end of a heaving line, and this nautical connection identifies well with Portsmouth as a seaport.

Eaton Lodge is a brick-built villa with a pierced parapet at first-floor level added later. The original part of the house is Gothic in style, including heavy dripstones above the first-floor windows, a style that is echoed by the later bay windows below.

Description

Built of dark red brick, using both Jacobean styling and that of the Arts and Crafts Movement, the house was designed by Edwin Lutyens to accommodate interiors removed from a property demolished in Bristol in the same year. The exterior is dominated by three-storey wings at each corner, creating an H-shaped plan, and the diagonally set chimneys that feature extensively in houses of this period. The rear elevation is far less formal, with Lutyens' trademark of juxtaposed dormer windows set into a long catslide roof and the

Location: Hampshire

Date: 1906–08

Type: Brick Jacobean-style house (Grade I)

The elaborate use of rubbed brickwork can be seen, especially on the projecting central porch which is topped by a trellis of brick. As on the whole house, the projecting entrance bay has casement-style leaded lights with rubbed brick mullions and rusticated quoins.

outbuildings showing his love of tiled detailing and small handmade bricks.

The interior is divided into the reclaimed rooms and those that Lutyens designed. The Bristol room was the original stateroom in an early seventeenth-century house and has a magnificent ceiling, chimney-piece and door-case. Outside this room is the staircase of the Bristol house with its elaborate carvings, which contrasts well with the simplicity of Lutyens own plans in the rest of the house.

History

John Langton built the Langton Mansion on Welsh Back in Bristol in 1623, and in recognition of becoming Mayor in 1628 had some lavish interiors added. The house remained a home until 1779, when it became part of a tobacco business that was subsequently bought in 1793 by George Franklyn, a member of a family of wealthy local merchants, and it remained a business until 1905. George Franklyn's grandson moved from Bristol in 1875 to live in Shedfield in Hampshire with his wife Annie and their three children. Over a period of fifty years Mr and Mrs Henry Franklyn contributed to the life of the community with philanthropic gestures such as building a reading room for the parish and commissioning the church spire. In 1904 Mrs Franklyn inherited the house in Bristol and, as it was due to be demolished, instructed the architect Edwin Lutyens to build New Place to house the interiors. The plaster ceilings, wooden panelling, fireplaces and staircase were carefully removed and transported from Bristol, firstly by rail and then by horsedrawn cart, to Shedfield.

New Place was named in recognition of a family link with Shakespeare (his house in Stratford was called New Place), and was built by J. Parnell and Sons of Rugby using handmade bricks from the Daneshill Brick and Tile Company at Basingstoke. When it was completed in 1908 Mrs Franklyn gave it to her son Captain Henry Franklyn as a wedding gift and it remained a family home until 1956, when it became a boys' preparatory school and, in 1978, a conference centre.

These architectural features were from the principal room of the Langton house. The chimney-piece features a Royal coat of arms, caryatids and columns, and the ceiling is a stunning example of strapwork, typical of town houses of the early seventeenth century.

The staircase was also removed from the seventeenth-century mansion. It is made primarily of oak with carved splat balusters and pierced pendants similar to those of the same period at Eyam Hall in Derbyshire.

The newel posts are topped with carved heraldic beasts, depicting the British Lion and Unicorn, a Welsh Dragon and a Griffin. The Bristol house had fewer beasts than were needed in the new house, so a local carpenter copied the carvings to complete the new staircase.

6. GARDEN HISTORY

Many small houses built before the nineteenth century had little in the way of a garden to cultivate in a frivolous fashion until the building of Georgian terraces in the eighteenth century and the introduction of gardening in the next century as a Victorian middle-class pastime. Land around early smaller rural dwellings was used for growing useful plants and, after the Enclosure Acts of the eighteenth and nineteenth centuries, available land became scarce for many households. What we now term as cottage gardens would have been packed with turnips rather than hollyhocks and, whatever the size of plot, all or part of it was used for growing edible and useful plants. These were tucked away out of sight on large country estates, but for smaller houses were planted anywhere a plant could be accommodated.

Where planned gardens did exist from the eighteenth century around medium-sized houses, it is likely that, as in house design, they were influenced by what the local landed gentry had in their garden or were a copied design from one of the contemporary pattern books. There are very few existing examples of small period gardens, therefore most sources in this chapter are from large estates. By studying the spaces around large period houses we can produce small-scale examples which, while not necessarily historically accurate for the house, will give a sense of the past. Most of us want to create an attractive and useful space that has overtones of history, and, just as most houses have elements from a number of periods, so gardens can have a blend of structures and plants from different eras. We can do this by looking at a range of historical sources and settings and understanding the elements that were important to that style.

Documentary sources for researching early gardens include manuscripts, plans, paintings, topographical pictures, historical pattern books

Hestercombe, Somerset This garden has several historical sections, including an eighteenth-century landscape, Victorian parterre and the inspired work of the partnership of Edwin Lutyens and Gertrude Jekyll, consisting of canals, fountains, raised walkways and a pergola.

and prints which show the layout of the space around a house. The backgrounds of early portraits give tantalizing glimpses of the land around grand houses and provide some insight into the design of early gardens. The earliest known English example is the portrait of Henry VIII and family with a view of the Great Garden of Whitehall Palace of around 1545. The painting shows a small fraction of the 23 acres (9ha) that the garden covered (almost four times that of Hampton Court), but it was some hundred years before the recording of gardens occurred in their own right. While work by gardeners like Lancelot 'Capability' Brown and Gertrude Jekyll is well documented, and there are surviving planting plans from large country estates, small cottage or town gardens are less likely to have original documentation and so historical accuracy needs to be found elsewhere.

Visits to gardens fall into categories ranging from historically accurate examples and re-creations, to gardens that have developed over

West Dean, West Sussex (Grade II) Pergola by Harold Peto (1912).

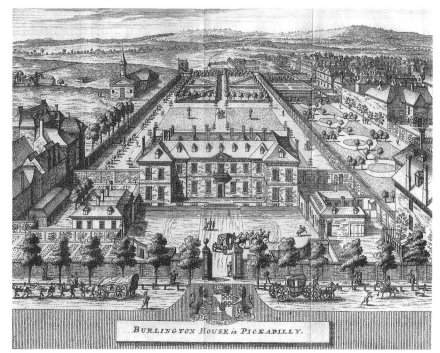

BURLINGTON HOUSE in PICKADILLY.

Burlington House, London (now the Royal Academy) *This print of 1707 shows the early formal walled gardens, complete with topiary and statues. The house was remodelled shortly afterwards, with the garden presumably receiving the same treatment.*

centuries with the influence of several designers and periods. The newly made garden surrounding 'Bayleaf Farmstead' (a fifteenth-century hall house rebuilt at the Weald & Downland Open Air Museum at Singleton) gives a flavour of how spaces around the house were used at that time and it includes practical plants such as vegetables and those for making medicines. Most of us would prefer a flower garden and we can discover from historical re-creations which plants were in England at the time the house was built and the way structure, planting and ornament was used. Many of the historical gardens that are open to the public surround large country

Bayleaf Garden, West Sussex *A re-creation of the space around this fifteenth-century farmhouse consists of woven wattle beds planted with vegetables and herbs indicative of the period.*

Nymans, West Sussex While retaining a sense of the past, the rose garden surrounded by yew hedges was redesigned in 1989. (By kind permission of the National Trust)

The Geffrye Museum, London The garden surrounding this museum is divided into rooms, each complementing one of the periods featured in the museum itself.

houses and are often divided into small 'rooms' that can be very influential to those designing a small traditional garden. Visiting a range of examples is the best way to understand the elements that make up a period garden. A basic knowledge of the styles of large gardens enables an informed choice of structures and plants to harmonize with a period house.

Early Influences

There has been an interest in cultivating our surroundings since the Roman occupation of Britain, where the gardens were enclosed spaces designed to grow both useful and decorative plants. With the Norman invasion came the introduction of woven willow arbours, turf-topped seats, mazes and raised beds with trellis.

They also brought with them exotic 'Moorish' influences from Spain, which developed during the following two centuries when the Crusaders brought back descriptions of foreign gardens. In the Middle Ages, gardens were known as *hortus conclusus*, meaning 'closed-off garden' and consisted of an enclosed 'flowery mead' or lawn, sown with perfumed flowers and surrounded by hedges, wattle fences or walls. The high walls of fortified buildings offered protection and formed ideal spaces to cultivate and gardens could only be safely made within monasteries and castles until the end of the Wars of the Roses in 1487. Haddon Hall in Derbyshire with its yew hedge and stone walls is an example of an enclosed garden of this time.

In the more peaceful Tudor period, gardens began to extend beyond the walls and

Great Dixter, East Sussex *Despite the sense of age, there was no garden here until 1912, when Lutyens and the owner, Nathaniel Lloyd, designed it around existing farm buildings to complement the manor house.*

Haddon Hall, Derbyshire *Of medieval origins, the terraced gardens below the long gallery were developed in the seventeenth century.*

Henry VIII, reigning from 1509, led the way in garden design, particularly in the use of the garden as an extension to living space as was common at that time in Italy. Garden buildings built for banqueting sprang up from his influence, as in the early octagonal brick example found at Melford Hall in Suffolk, built in 1560, and at Eyam Hall in Derbyshire a little later. Architectural features were important in Tudor gardens such as sundials and 'King's Beasts' (carved heraldic animals mounted on poles), the forerunners of garden statuary. There was an increased interest in botany, with books published on the subject, and flowers became a common inspiration for decorative motifs for both the interiors and exteriors of buildings. The Tudor period is synonymous with symmetry and pattern, often in the form of topiary (the shaping of trees and hedges) and knot gardens, in which designs were created from knots expressed as low-growing hedges with flowering plants or coloured earth in-between. Gardens were still enclosed with stone or brick walls and the knot gardens in some cases became a pattern of low shrubs called a 'maze'. Although mazes had been around for thousands of years in various guises,

Ludlow, Shropshire *This timber shows the use of floral detailing on the exterior of a building, a sign of the first owner's wealth.*

Basing House, Hampshire *Recently laid out in the style of the early seventeenth century, this parterre is enclosed by brick walls and corner gazebos.*

Montecute, Somerset *The layout of the north garden dates from the late sixteenth century and includes a raised walkway. The planting, including the Irish yews, is nineteenth century. One of two stone gazebos overlooking the original east entrance can be seen on the left. (By kind permission of the National Trust)*

during the Tudor period they were built to be of interest visually and were sometimes made to be viewed from above, as at Hatfield in Hertfordshire. A further development was the high-hedged maze designed as a puzzle (possibly of Dutch origin and often referred to as a labyrinth), with an early example at Nonsuch Palace recorded in the 1580s.

During Elizabeth I's reign a great number of new and exotic plants and vegetables arrived from abroad, coupled with a vast number of new houses being built and gardens laid. This was an exciting time for those interested in gardens who were wealthy enough to indulge their passion, and Elizabeth encouraged garden-making among her courtiers. The gardens were still divided into sections, with a geometrical base as before, but they were even more elaborate than in her father's reign and included a greater number of statues, buildings and fountains. The

Forde Abbey, Somerset *A rectangular living 'Beech House' is in the grounds of this converted monastery.*

building of terraces allowed far-reaching views of the garden and made a strong link with the house, as can be seen at Montecute House in Somerset. Raised mounts for viewing the garden, often topped by a protected seat, and living arbours were also popular during the sixteenth and seventeenth centuries. Lawns started to appear around this time (made sometimes of camomile) to sit upon or for bowling, a pastime made famous by Francis Drake. However, it was during the Jacobean and Stuart period that the close-cut English lawn was achieved and envied by the rest of Europe.

While Tudor gardens were founded on medieval ideas, the influences of Italy encouraged a greater use of geometry in the relationship between house and garden and in the designs of parterres and water features. The first Italianate garden to be made in England was at Wilton House in Wiltshire in 1633. Many of these early gardens were later redesigned or lost during the Civil War, but, once Charles II was on the throne, interest in gardens revived. In major towns, the early seventeenth century saw the beginning of enclosed residential squares, initially being formed as part of the Enclosure Acts. Covent Garden was the first in London, completed in 1639. It was created from land confiscated from the Church during the Dissolution of the Monasteries and consisted of a patch of grass surrounded by terraces of houses. These early squares were turfed, but, when influenced in the eighteenth century by the fashions and by Acts of Parliament, most were redesigned with symmetrical beds, trees and gravel. The harmonious balance of flower beds, coupled with ornamentation in the form of trelliswork and classical lead or stone statuary, continued to be important in all types of gardens.

During the seventeenth century several botanical gardens were established, including the Apothecaries' Garden in Chelsea in 1673 (now known as Chelsea Physic Garden) to train apprentices in plant identification and to study new plants imported into England. Design influences were still from France and Italy, although, due to the differences in the natural contours of

Melbourne Hall, Derbyshire *Thomas Coke inherited this estate in 1696, and, having studied garden design in France, set about its remodelling, adding statues, water features and yew hedges. The original plan survives, as does information about the 'birdcage' made by the famous ironsmith Robert Bakewell in circa 1710 for £120.*

Eyam, Derbyshire *A late seventeenth-century H-shaped façade, with walled front entrance garden.*

the land and high costs involved, many English gardens were less elaborate than their European counterparts. Melbourne Hall in Derbyshire is a late seventeenth-century example of the use of statuary, vistas and water, but, while the major influence in this garden is French, the late seventeenth-century gardeners had found new inspiration in the gardens of Holland. The Dutch influence was due partly to William and Mary's accession to the English throne in 1688, but also as a result of Holland's excellent trade routes bringing ideas from further afield. However, Dutch gardens were as flat as the French ones, so these ideas still had to be adapted to the English 'landscape', a word also brought over from Holland. Dutch influence and their developments in water technology brought canals and garden vistas to English gardens, as can be seen at Westbury Court in Gloucestershire and these grand statements were the precursor to the next stage in garden history.

The Georgian Landscape Garden

A significant change in style occurred at the beginning of the eighteenth century, bringing a less formal vision to large gardens. Moving away from the symmetrical topiary of the previous century, the new style allowed shrubs and trees

Chiswick House, Surrey Designed by William Kent in the 1720s for Lord Burlington, this garden has a mixture of formal vistas near the house and a more informal landscape beyond. (By kind permission of English Heritage)

The Painswick Rococo Garden, Gloucestershire The Rococo style, a whimsical aside to the landscape tradition, is epitomized in the design of this garden of the 1740s, complete with an array of garden buildings, such as the Eagle House, restored with the help of paintings of the newly laid garden by Thomas Robins.

to grow naturally. The early formally laid gardens disappeared under a natural-looking rolling landscape, which was really the result of a lengthy and labour-intensive remodelling of the land with vast lakes, wandering pathways and temples, as can be seen at Hestercombe in Somerset. Country estates also had kitchen gardens separated from the park by walls, where food and flowering plants were grown for use in the house. Later in the century, Stowe, in Buckinghamshire, had its kitchen garden remodelled by young Lancelot 'Capability' Brown. Brown went on to develop his own 'landscape style', which offered no eye-catching adornments in the form of ruins or bridges, and for this reason many late eighteenth-century country houses may seem to have little architectural relationship with the surrounding landscape.

As well as landscaping grand estates, landowners were able to rearrange the lives of their tenants, with cottages, gardens and village greens often part of the scheme. Far from being an altruistic gesture, sometimes the reason a new village was built was that the original was unattractive, or inconveniently placed too close to the country seat. The practice of emparking allowed the village to be rebuilt a safe distance

Milton Abbas, Dorset *This designed estate of the 1770s was the work of Sir William Chambers and Lancelot 'Capability' Brown.*

away in a fashionable style, adding to the picturesque qualities of the landscape. Nuneham Courtney in Oxfordshire in the 1760s and Milton Abbas in Dorset a decade later are both examples of the whim of landowners; at Milton Abbas the landowner employed 'Capability' Brown to oversee the improvements.

Humphrey Repton, like Brown, was not trained in design and was the first to use the term 'landscape gardener'. He supported the inclusion of certain architectural elements to link the house to the landscape and reintroduced the use of the Elizabethan terrace into his designs, marrying interior and exterior space. His *Red Books* (around 400 were produced) included overlapping 'before and after' paintings of the garden scheme. Unlike some of his contemporaries, Repton allowed owners to have small flower gardens close to the house and buildings from which to view elements of the landscape. A gazebo, likely to be a derivation of the words 'gaze about', was sometimes built in order to view the surrounding landscape, an idea reminiscent of Tudor garden buildings and often copied in smaller gardens. Repton took ideas from a number of schools of thought including the picturesque style, which required each view to be as interesting as a painting, with a focal point, such as a ruin, bridge or temple. He produced a mixture of landscape ideas that contained references from

many parts of the world and allowed well-travelled and enthusiastic landowners to use their knowledge of foreign places. With the mass of influences streaming from the continent and architects, designers and estate gardeners on 'The Grand Tour', the nineteenth century had become a tremendous mixture of styles. Repton's oriental water garden at Seizincote in Gloucestershire surrounds a house in the Indian style, and a love of anything 'exotic' continued throughout the century. 'Chinoiserie' and Indian interiors of the Regency Period found their way into the garden with whimsical summer houses and exotic seating. The fashion for the

The Gazebo Garden, Hampshire *Built in the rear garden of a provincial Georgian town house, this gazebo, dated 1779, is now surrounded by a small re-created period garden. It originally overlooked fields.*

The Great Exhibition Catalogue (1851) Examples of garden furniture made from wood were soon copied in cheaper materials, with exhibitions such as this one encouraging the proliferation of styles.

picturesque was still evident and included a 'rustic' look used for summer houses and garden furniture, as was displayed at the 1851 Great Exhibition in Hyde Park.

Small Eighteenth-Century Gardens

Owners of large estates could remodel to suit every new style, but small houses in towns, often on the original medieval plot system, had little space for an elaborate garden. In the country, the Enclosure Acts had changed the right to use common land and cottagers had to make do with the patch around the house to grow the family food. This tradition continued in many places until at least the 1930s (and also after the Second World War in some areas), when council houses were built with large back gardens to encourage tenants to grow their own vegetables.

Town gardens first appeared in London in the 1720s, although initially it was an upper-class innovation in places like Mayfair. In these long, thin plots there was an historical reference to the gardens of the sixteenth century, where trellis, geometrical shapes and shaped trees were used to divide the space and to continue the symmetry of the house. The garden surface tended to be gravel or the more expensive stone paving (as opposed to grass), with the addition of planters and pots, the most common elements in a garden

up to the early nineteenth century. Widely spaced wooden fencing was used to divide small gardens both in towns and villages, with brick being used only to enclose the gardens of the rather more grand houses until brick making expanded to industrial proportions in the nineteenth century. Georgian town gardens were formal spaces, and architectural features such as pedimented arches and obelisks were used to create a focal point furthest from the house, in the way that temples did for Repton's rolling acres.

Although gardens were designed to improve the view from the house and to obscure service areas, there were some owners who took a greater interest in gardening, seeking help from early gardening journals and books on planting and layout. Advice offered was often conflicting. Some writers of the time felt that plants would not survive in such polluted places as towns and that paving the entire garden was the only course of action. There were those who disputed this and the first plantsman's book, *City Gardener* by Thomas Fairchild (1722), indicated that many plants and trees would thrive in the town garden. Styles and fashions popular in London soon travelled to towns in the south-east and beyond, though they often took many months or years to become established around the country.

Bath, Somerset *The enclosed garden and the houses that surround it were built by John Straham in 1727–36 and represent the period before town houses of this kind had their own gardens.*

Bath, Somerset *This is a re-creation of a garden behind one of John Wood the Younger's town houses found during an archaeological excavation and it represents the original plan of circa 1760. The planting scheme is representative of the period and includes topiary, fragrant climbers and fruit trees.*

Spa towns, such as Leamington and Bath, quickly followed London in the fashion for town gardens and communal squares. Many early Georgian town houses were not designed with individual gardens, but shared a communal one, an example being Queen Square (1728–29) built in Bath by John Wood the Elder. By the 1750s it had become fashionable to have individual gardens, and houses built by John Wood the Younger included not only private gardens, but also landscaped open communal areas linking the streets. An excellent example of a restored Georgian garden (circa 1760) can be found behind Number Four, The Circus, in Bath and another is re-created at Pickfords House

Museum in Derby. Towards the end of the eighteenth century formal front gardens started to appear in London's wider new streets of Kensington, Islington and Lambeth, although most examples of this were built over to become shop fronts in the next century.

The Beginning of Gardening for the Masses

As new styles and ideas emerged, more and more architects showed an interest in designing the land around their houses. John Claudius Loudon was one of this new breed of architect, admiring the formal gardens abroad and the naturalistic visions of Repton, but with innovative ideas of his own. In 1832 he coined the phrase 'Gardenesque', in which plants could be left in their natural shapes, but the plant-centred garden was to be recognizable as the work of man, not nature. He was a new type of designer for a new kind of garden and this was to prove to be the beginning of gardening as a national pursuit. Loudon designed public spaces such as Derby Arboretum, which opened in 1840 (currently being restored), but he is known more for his writings on gardening and garden design than its practice. He responded to the needs of the owners of average-sized gardens and was aware that the increasing interest in gardening was from a wider social group, only some of whom had their own gardeners. Loudon's 'Gardenesque' style was reinterpreted for suburban garden proportions and, for these more modest gardeners, books and magazines soon became easily available, tailored to suit the average needs. Loudon's *The Suburban Gardener and Villa Companion* (1838) categorized gardens into 'rates' in a similar way that the Building Act of 1774 did for houses. However, Loudon's rates related more to the location and amount of land available than to the size of house for which the garden was designed. Articles in *The Gardener's Magazine*, first published in 1825, encouraged more informal planting schemes, and by 1835 the magazine was advocating the use of grass instead of gravel and the extensive use of dark evergreens.

Edensor, Derbyshire
*Stone villas built in the
1840s to house the
Chatsworth estate
workers are set in wide
green spaces with their
own cottage gardens.*

This was the beginning of the Victorian garden, which became a fully blown pastime for the Victorian middle classes. There were still strong regional differences in the use of town plots and many small houses in overcrowded towns had no outside space. Certain towns such as Nottingham were famous for allotments rather than flower gardens. By the end of the nineteenth century, new houses in fashionable towns were not only being built with secluded rear gardens, but often included front gardens. Sometimes optical tricks were employed to create a greater sense of space and to mimic a front garden, as can be seen at Brunswick Square, Sussex, where there was a central garden and an uninterrupted view of the sea. Smaller versions sprang up in other locations, and the building of John Nash's Regents Park Villages East and West, begun in 1826 with their individual hedged front gardens, was perhaps a step towards the modern suburban garden. By the middle of the century, in London and in other fashionable cities, private communal squares had ceased to be built and parks had started to

Leamington Spa, Warwickshire *Built in the 1830s,
these paired villas surround a circular road with a
central private garden, offering a pleasant view from
verandas and typical of the period.*

Southsea, Hampshire *Southsea Common was
purchased from the War Department and its beds
laid out in 1922, although the style is reminiscent of
carpet bedding of the previous century.*

become truly public, rather than the tantalizing private spaces of the previous century.

By the middle of the nineteenth century, there was a return to the symmetry of earlier centuries in the use of geometric flower beds called parterres (often referred to as carpet bedding), designed to be viewed from above. This legacy can still be seen in many public parks today. This was also the beginning of the formal opening of private gardens to the public and one of the first was Elvaston Castle in Derbyshire in 1851, which sparked a renewed interest in topiary. In large gardens mazes also saw a revival, such as the holly maze planted at Castle Bromwich Gardens in 1890 and the yew maze planted in 1840 at Hatfield House.

By the twentieth century, costs related to the keeping of formal gardens were becoming prohibitive, increased wages and the loss of many gardeners, particularly after the First World War, required more practical cottage styles. Large Victorian gardens had used many gardeners, sometimes changing whole beds of plants at night under the cover of darkness, much to the surprise of waking guests. Despite technological innovations this sort of extravagance became more unusual, although there were still some owners of large country houses who had the interest and wealth to employ garden designers. The gardens at Melbourne Hall in Derbyshire were restored during this period and West Dean Gardens in Sussex added some Italianate features to the earlier landscaped space.

Increased wealth in the middle classes and speculative builders with the latest architectural pattern books created a mass of revivals of

West Dean, West Sussex *In the last decade of the nineteenth century, Harold Peto was commissioned to make alterations to the house and garden, culminating in the 300ft (90m) long colonnaded pergola and gazebo (1912). (By kind permission of the West Dean Estate)*

Barrington Court, Somerset *Surrounding this Elizabethan manor house, the garden was restored in the 1920s under the influence of Gertrude Jekyll. It now consists of several small walled rooms with intersecting herringbone-patterned brick paths that contrast well with the limestone of the house. (By kind permission of The National Trust)*

English architecture which required complementary gardens. Lawns that for centuries had been labour-intensive became affordable for the Victorian suburban garden after the invention of the lawnmower, patented in 1832. The Arts and Crafts garden sprang from John Claudius Loudon's theories of the natural, coupled with the return to all things medieval advocated by influential people such as John Ruskin and William Morris. Far from the well-tended knot gardens one would assume to fit well with the medieval ideal, the true Arts and Crafts garden is a mass of riotous colour and pattern, swathes of herbaceous planting and a considered use of foliage. Garden designer William Robinson grasped Loudon's ideas, and with a passionate hatred of Victorian carpet bedding, encouraged the use of foliage plants that could be grouped naturally.

Rodmarton, Gloucestershire *Ernest Barnsley designed both the house and much of the garden at the beginning of the twentieth century. The garden was built as the house took shape and was designed as a series of rooms bordered by walls or hedges and included garden buildings such as the stone summer house. (© S. Biddulph)*

Hestercombe, Somerset *The Edwardian pergola, with its 'claire-voies' (oval windows) at each end, extends the garden by providing a view of the surrounding countryside.*

Although there were a number of architects of the period who designed gardens in tandem with the house, such as Ernest Barnsley, it is the influence of the later partnership of Gertrude Jekyll and Edwin Lutyens that comes to mind when gardens of this period are considered. Jekyll specialized in cottage gardening, having been brought up in an unspoilt village in Surrey and having attended art school at the height of the Arts and Crafts Movement. These early influences, coupled with the study of gardens in Italy, clearly gave her an understanding of the relationship between architecture, plants and colour theory. This mixture of designer and plantswoman, alongside her partnership with Lutyens, was to create some of the most wonderful gardens in existence. Her ideas can be seen in a number of gardens, such as Hestercombe in Somerset and several others that can be visited through the National Gardens Scheme. Although Jekyll gardens have a strong personal style, when left to his own devices Lutyens was able to design gardens in a range of styles to suit client and plot, as seen at Castle Drogo in Devon and in his contribution to Hampstead Garden Suburb in London.

The outskirts of major cities seemed the most logical place to build new houses and the vision of the garden suburb was started in the 1870s at Bedford Park in London. The housing situation was ripe for new ideas and the public's interest in gardening, coupled with improved transport systems, meant that landscaped developments of suburban dwellings with private gardens could be created. The example at Hampstead in London in 1906 was based on the vision of a medieval village, growing from within the surrounding landscape, using existing trees to help the houses blend in. Much of the landscaping of the suburbs showed a return to the landscape ideas of the eighteenth century in the use of winding paths, roads and vistas.

Garden cities were influenced not only by the ideas of the Arts and Crafts Movement, but by the model villages of the previous century. These workers' units were on a scale far larger than any seen before, and the best gardens are at Saltaire and New Earswick in Yorkshire and Bournville in Birmingham. Saltaire, a complete textile mill town built from the 1850s, had its own park and the plots included gardens of varying size depending on the status of the factory worker. Built some fifty years later, the layout of the gardens at Bournville were given as much attention as the houses, as George Cadbury, the cocoa factory owner, was a keen gardener. Fruit trees, vegetable plots and a lawn were included, and gardening was seen as the ideal hobby for a factory worker. Joseph Rowntree's effort at New Earswick had all the

Bournville, West Midlands *George Cadbury's estate was designed and built by 1900. It allowed for both private gardens and wide open green spaces and was a far cry from the typical housing for workers of the time.*

Castle Bromwich Gardens, West Midlands The garden was developed during the late seventeenth century and has been restored to include a raised walk and a nineteenth-century holly maze. The Green House was built circa 1729 along with the brick walls that enclose the garden, and features the family coat of arms, the English lion and other classical details.

elements of Bournville, with generous open spaces and tree-lined roads. These early new towns and suburbs set guidelines for town planning and for the first time ensured that green space and private gardens were essential elements of every scheme, until changes in mass housing came in the 1960s.

Garden Buildings and Glasshouses

Glasshouses have been important in gardens for centuries, for growing fruit, keeping exotic plants and for extending the house space. Their importance has fluctuated and their role altered, with changing fashions and building innovations making them more accessible to a wider spectrum of people. Having been designed and built

in Europe as early as the fourteenth century, the use of glasshouses for botanical study did not develop in England until 1621, on the land of the University of Oxford. Two more botanical gardens in London and Edinburgh followed some fifty years later. Interesting new plants continued to arrive throughout the seventeenth century and gardeners employed by the aristocracy travelled abroad in search of unusual plants. John Tradescant, one of the earliest garden designers, having laid out the gardens at Hatfield House, returned from foreign travels with such exotics as the Yucca and the Tulip Tree. Interest surged in plants grown for their foliage which were planted in tubs. These were called 'greens' and were over-wintered in 'greenhouses', hence the name we all recognize.

Orangeries and greenhouses became more popular, as the glass manufacturers of the eighteenth century were better able to produce flat panes of quality. Fruit such as peaches, apricots, nectarines and other citrus fruit were grown in these glasshouses. Pineapple was a high-status fruit, popular within the upper classes by 1750. At the Lost Gardens of Heligan in Cornwall, they have restored their early pineapple pits, demonstrating the method for keeping the fruit warm using fermenting compost. Early in the eighteenth century, orangeries were designed to be extra living spaces in summer and a place in which to take walks in bad weather, as at Chatsworth in Derbyshire. There was a distinction made between conservatories for display and glasshouses for growing, and there were innovative developments in heating, ventilation and overall design of these buildings during the eighteenth century. Travel around the world had increased the number of exotic plants available, although most were housed in glasshouses or in the kitchen gardens, rather than featured in the garden where the bright colours would detract from the natural qualities of the landscape.

By 1800 the ridged greenhouse had been devised; an early example can be seen at Bicton Park, Devon (1820). The Royal Horticultural Society was formed in 1804 at Kew Gardens. It organized seasoned travellers to collect specimens from abroad and in 1841 Queen Victoria gave the collection to the nation. By 1838 conservatories were being used more as areas to grow plants than purely as outdoor living spaces. The best examples are the Palm House at Kew (1844–48) and Sir Joseph Paxton's Victoria Regia Lily House at Chatsworth, completed in 1849, where the cast-iron pillars were positioned to allow a carriage to be driven through. These magnificent examples encouraged the general public to have versions of their own and to visit the newly popular 'winter gardens' that sprang up all around the country. During this period

West Dean, West Sussex *The walled kitchen gardens were moved to their present position out of sight of the house in 1804, and contain glasshouses to grow figs, peaches, nectarines and grapes. Heated initially by the hot-bed method, coal had taken over by the middle of the nineteenth century. (By kind permission of the West Dean Estate)*

Southsea, Hampshire *Conservatories designed for the Victorian domestic market could be as highly decorated as the house, and this first-floor example includes stained glass and ornamental brattishing.*

there was immense botanical interest in the way that the plants were laid out and labelled, and manufacturers saw a market for conservatories for middle-class homes.

The interest in the conservatory at this time was similar to the fashion for orangeries a century before and was due to a number of factors. There was a rise in the wealth of middle-class households, a reduction in the cost of glass caused by the repeal of the tax on glass in 1851, and the technology was available to produce affordable prefabricated metal-frame construction, enabling conservatories to be priced to sell. The popularity of the Victorian conservatory must also in some way be attributed to the building in 1851 of the Exhibition Hall in Hyde Park, later termed 'The Crystal Palace'. It was produced off site to a modular design, only took sixteen months to complete and lasted over eighty years before it was destroyed by fire in 1936. Typical conservatories of the Victorian period had low brick walls, wooden mullioned windows with straight glass and a pitched glass roof sometimes using cast-iron supports. Plants grown for their foliage became popular during this time and as a result 'ferneries' were built to house the collections of tender examples.

Conservatories could be attached to the house in a number of ways and not all were full size. Rooftop, balcony or corridor conservatories suited those with less space, and were available due to the ease with which the ready-made components could be adapted to fit any situation. A conservatory became an 'essential addition to the Victorian House', especially in the residential parts of London and other cities, and the Edwardian period saw continued enjoyment of these structures. The eventual decline of the conservatory was caused by high maintenance costs, fuel shortage during the First World War and, in the larger versions, a lack of gardeners to maintain the plants, along with renewed interest in outdoor gardening. Between the wars, the conservatory at Chatsworth was demolished due to problems with glazing and its maintenance costs, and, with the loss of The Crystal Palace, two of Joseph Paxton's greatest buildings had gone and,

Hay-on-Wye, Herefordshire Glassed areas were fitted into houses in strange places, as can be seen here between the roof and the chimney stack.

by the end of the Second World War, so had all interest in conservatories. Contrary to this, there was a surge of interest in more practical greenhouses during the Second World War, with many people growing their own produce to supplement family rations. It was to take a quarter of a century before another generation saw the desirability of conservatories as extensions of living spaces and these, in common with the eighteenth-century versions, generally have little to do with plants.

Planning a Period Garden

To begin your research find books about the period or periods in which you are most interested, and follow this with visits to both period gardens and inspirational contemporary examples. From your reading and visits, select one or two key design features of the period to use as a central theme and build up the garden around these chosen period features. Garden buildings have played a large part in garden design for centuries, but consider scale and detail to avoid them dominating your plot. Bear in mind the aspects of the garden you enjoy now and consider keeping elements that may have been part of the garden for some time.

As an accurate reconstruction of your garden is unlikely to be possible, allow individual preferences to dictate the choice of plants and consider how the existing garden can be developed, rather than erased. A Tudor-inspired garden may evolve from a direct influence such as low box hedging, but include motifs from later centuries. Creating a garden with an Arts and Crafts influence will be more about the plants chosen and the way they are juxtaposed, than any rigid planned structure of paths and statues. Some plants that featured in early gardens do not thrive now due to the change in climate over the past 500 years, so take advice if you want to include early plants. Conversely, as our climate is generally warmer, some plants introduced into England for conservatories will now survive being planted outside. Consider commissioning special items like gates, planters and seats with a sense of the period from a designer-craftsman, rather than a reproduction or reclaimed version. Unlike interior design, gardens need time to mature to realize their full potential and are designed for the benefit of future owners.

West Dean, West Sussex *The nineteenth-century Sunken Garden is designed in the picturesque style, with raised beds of drystone walling and four thatched summer houses. (By kind permission of the West Dean Estate)*

Heligan, Cornwall *This restoration project can be useful to owners of small gardens as it is divided into small spaces, like the Italian Garden with a pool and summer house enclosed by laurel hedges, which was restored with the aid of a photograph from 1909.*

Walmer Castle, Kent *The gardens around the converted Tudor fortifications have developed over the last 200 years, culminating in this celebration of the Queen Mother's ninety-fifth birthday by Penelope Hobhouse. (By kind permission of English Heritage)*

Description

Brunswick Square is laid out on three sides of a sloping site facing south to the seafront across a large communal garden. The houses are of five different designs but, despite being built by many builders, there is a unified feeling about this speculative development which is a testament to the control of the development's architects. The houses are between three and five storeys high, of rendered brick under slate roofs, built directly on to the pavement and were designed to rival the town houses of London and Bath. The common elements in the houses

Location: East Sussex

Date: 1825–27

Type: Regency Terrace
               (Grade I)

The façades of the houses on Brunswick Square differ depending on where they are in Busby's grand scheme. All the windows should be of the small-paned variety, but some were replaced during the Victorian period.

Brunswick Square

are the use of rusticated stucco on the ground floor, the mansard roof hidden behind a parapet, the use of cast-iron railings and balconies and elegantly proportioned sash windows with glazing bars. The five variations in the houses include two types of bow fronts, the use of columns, engaged columns and pilasters, parapet balustrades and triangular caps above some windows. The interiors were designed with piped water and flushing toilets, but, as each house was built for a particular client, differences in layout and detail are apparent.

The façade of Number Thirteen is a gentle bow pierced by three sash windows on each level, with full-height versions for the first-floor drawing room or 'piano nobile' and pilasters emphasizing this important room. A cast-iron balcony at this level and railings on the ground floor with steps to the front door complete the design.

Once inside, the plan equates to a 'first rate' house as stipulated by the 1774 London Building Act and comprises five floors and a basement.

History

Charles Augustin Busby and Amon Wilds designed Brunswick Town, a small Regency enclave in Hove, for wealthy clients, just as Thomas Kemp did in Brighton. Speculative builders built Brunswick Square to Busby's design using quality materials and it became the highlight of the development. Number Ten (originally Number Eight) was built by local builders Thomas Cooper and Charles Lynn for Sir Robert Cunynghame and his wife, who lived there from 1827 until 1841. On their deaths it passed to their daughter and was sold in 1869 to Mr Henry Hawkes, a Justice of the Peace. Cooper and Lynn also built Number Thirteen and by 1881 Phoebe Wardell, an elderly lady with four servants, was residing there. Other occupants of the terrace at the time of the census included physicians, members of the legal profession and clergy.

The Regency Town House at Number 13 Brunswick Square (and the basement of Number 10) is currently being restored, but is open to the public by appointment. For further information, go to www.Regency-town-house.org.uk.

This is a bow-fronted example and the piano nobile on the first floor is emphasized by the large engaged Corinthian columns and a cast-iron balcony, which contrasts well with the strong cream of the painted stucco.

Within the development there was a choice of stone or wooden staircases and at Number Thirteen, seen here, the dog-leg staircase that gently rises in the popular fashion from an elegant hall is timber with a cast-iron balustrade and mahogany handrail.

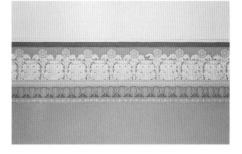

All the plasterwork at Number Thirteen has been beautifully restored, including cornices and ceiling roses, and is now being painted in colours found during the process. In the dining room, the walls and plasterwork are painted shades of purple, a colour believed to aid the digestion of Regency diners.

7. BUYING AND LEGISLATION

In 1877 the Society for the Protection of Ancient Buildings was founded and this formed the catalyst for the preservation of buildings of architectural and historical merit, which in turn led to a number of Acts of Parliament. The Town and Country Planning Acts of 1944 and 1947 initiated a twenty-year survey of all buildings in England and Wales, which created the first list of buildings of special architectural and historical interest. A reappraisal began in 1970, after some revision of the criteria, and in the last twenty years a further consideration, of the age and type of buildings added to the list, has been undertaken. Buildings are included on the list and approved by the Secretary of State because they have an importance historically or architecturally. This can be an individual listing of a building or a group listing within a small area such as a village or street, and, in addition to houses, the list contains a racing-pigeon loft, hundreds of pigsties and two ventilation shafts in the Blackwall Tunnel. All buildings that were built before 1700 and are in a reasonably original condition are listed, as are most structures built before 1840. After this date, tighter criteria are presented and considerations such as rarity in style or materials, connection with an historical figure or event, or the work of a named architect, are all possible reasons for these later buildings to be listed. In England and Wales only 2 per cent of all buildings are listed; this is currently around 360,000, of which only a proportion were designed as houses or are still used as such.

Listed buildings fall into three categories: 92 per cent are Grade II and represent important buildings of special interest; the other 8 per cent are made up of Grade II*, which are outstanding buildings, sometimes with regional importance, and a few buildings of exceptional and often

Hove, East Sussex (Grade I) The Brunswick development (circa 1820) is Grade I listed to preserve the unity of the whole design and because of the many significant residents who have lived in the square.

national importance are given Grade I status. The purpose of listing a building is to protect it from being demolished, altered in an unsympathetic or inappropriate way, or from having important features removed. The list contains the details known about a building and may include both the exterior and interior details. However, the protection that listed status affords covers every architectural feature of the building and its immediate surroundings, regardless of

Rye, East Sussex (Grade II) Originally an independent chapel and dated 1817, this building has since been converted for domestic use.

whether they are specifically mentioned. In 2001 requests were put forward to demolish a total of 221 listed buildings in England and Wales, some having been damaged by fire and one or two that had already been demolished, the biggest number within one area being in Liverpool. An owner of a listed building has legal liabilities that are explained in The Planning (Listed Buildings and Conservation Areas) Act of 1990, and all three types of listing have the same degree of protection from demolition or alteration.

If you have bought, or are considering buying, a listed property or one in a conservation area, there are certain responsibilities that go with ownership. You do not have the right to alter or remove features in a listed house without permission, and boundary walls, outbuildings and other exterior structures may come under the listed status. Any repairs must be undertaken on a 'like for like' basis and the council can serve a Repairs Notice on any owner failing to maintain the property adequately. A previously unlisted house can become listed during ownership in one of two ways. It can be recommended for listing by an individual or an authoritative body, or as a result of a new survey carried out by the local authority. The spot listing of houses is rare and although some autonomy will be taken

away from you with regard to altering your house, there is a positive side. If your house does become listed it is likely to be more saleable, as many house hunters value a listed property above others.

In addition to the statutory list, many local authorities and borough councils keep their own lists of buildings in their area of particular local significance and an unlisted house may be included on this list. Although this does not give the same protection, the building will be considered more carefully in the event of a suggested change that requires standard planning permission. Conservation areas are places of special historical or architectural interest and were created in 1967, starting with Stamford in

Tettenhall, West Midlands (Grade II) This ogee-topped trellised porch, Gothic fanlight, double door and railings will all be part of the listing of this pretty nineteenth-century house.

Westfield, East Sussex (Grade II) This farmhouse is given standard protection, but, despite being older than its datestone of 1690, it may not have enough significant features left to warrant greater protection.

Lincolnshire, and there are now over 8,000 in England. The buildings within such an area are protected in a similar way to listed status, with a particular concern for the visual effect on the area that alterations on one building might create. Councils have different requirements for conservation areas and in addition can withdraw normal permitted development rights (Article 4 Directions) to alterations that are inappropriate to the locality. Buildings in conservation areas are not subject to the same internal constraints as those that are listed, but if you wish to alter the exterior you will need to submit a request to the local council in a similar way to applying for listed building consent. Boundaries of conservation areas are regularly reviewed and buildings can become part of a conservation area as a result.

Buying a Period House

Owners of period houses need to have a genuine love of old properties and to accept that they are guardians of part of the country's heritage. They need to have an understanding of the way houses have evolved, their styles and the technological advances that have occurred and be prepared to seek specialist advice from appropriate sources. Owners have a responsibility to maintain the property in good order and to make repairs as sympathetically as possible. In many cases, listed status lends legal weight to this task, although only in the Grade I category can you expect some sort of financial support. If you resent having to share your home with specialists, enthusiasts or conservation officers, a listed home may not be the right choice for you. For example, if you own a house designed by a well-known architect you may be expected to open your home to historians from time to time, but there is a benefit to you as professionals can offer you further knowledge and advice about your house. Architectural historians can help to interpret the important aspects of the house and, in this informed way, owners can make decisions concerning the restoration of details and the general upkeep of the structure. In most cases, while

maintaining the fabric and special architectural features, a house can continue to be sensitively adapted, as many have been over the centuries. Conservation officers have different ways of interpreting the listing status of a house, and those who are happy to see sympathetic development know that it is only by being lived in that period houses are ensured a continued existence.

Restored listed houses are now much more commonly advertised than the neglected examples, as 'makeover' and 'house history' programmes have created a surge in interest in updating properties. Houses in need of restoration, whether listed or not, are becoming rare in many parts of the country, and it is now unusual to find a dream cottage to restore in a perfect location. If you are prepared to search a wide area and have an open mind about the sort of property you want, then you are much more likely to have a choice. Houses that have been

Shere, Surrey (Grade II) *This lodge, built in 1894, is a pretty house in a picturesque village, but its listing is more about having being designed by the architect Edwin Lutyens.*

lived in by tenants for some time or owned by estates as workers' cottages are usually very interesting to restore. While they have usually been adequately maintained, they are less likely to have been victims of fashion and expensive alterations, with the result that many original features may lie behind hardboard or wallpaper. The biggest collection of period houses is Victorian, but houses up to the 1960s are now considered old enough to be of a 'significant period', so an even larger pool of houses has become available for restoration.

In most major towns and cities there are interesting older properties that do not have individual protection from listed status and are not in a conservation area. A period house with no restrictions or status can mean that, subject to standard planning rules, you can alter and adapt in whatever way you like. However, this apparently free hand does mean that you may not have access to local expertise, and also does not give you the incentive to research appropriate methods and materials or to find out how the house has developed. All major estate agents will have period properties on their books, but some specialize in older houses and sometimes, more particularly, those that are listed. Those that specialize in period properties tend to use websites to advertise and there are two types of site to

Emsworth, Hampshire *This 1920s bungalow retains many of its important original features, such as the correct fenestration, and later additions have blended well into the design.*

view, those commercially based and the charitable ones. Charities tend to concentrate on 'Buildings at Risk', and in some cases a fee is required to register and look at the database of buildings. Anyone interested in old buildings will find all the websites listed very interesting, even if they have no intention of purchasing. A Building at Risk (BaR) is an historically important building which is sometimes in need of substantial repairs. The 'At Risk' registers of SAVE, English Heritage and the Society for the Protection of Ancient Buildings are full of interesting buildings, many in need of a thoughtful owner with ample funds to lavish on a property of this sort. Unfortunately, they are not always in a suitable location or indeed available to purchase. English Heritage seems to concentrate on highlighting important Grade II* and Grade I buildings, most of which are in the restoration process, but, as they account for one in twenty-seven of all buildings in this category, will remain on the register until completion. Building Preservation Trusts are charitable organizations set up to buy buildings at risk and restore them, financed through the Architectural Heritage Fund. In some cases, the building is then sold on the open market or leased for an intended purpose. These trusts are usually a last resort for a building at risk and are therefore not in direct competition with private individuals.

Auctions can be a good way to buy a house that needs work or is unusual, making valuation difficult for the vendor. In the past, this was a cost-effective way to purchase, but this seems less likely now that many more of us are looking for the same type of house. You will be up against developers and cash buyers and will have to be ready to complete on the purchase very soon after the auction. Searches and surveys need to be completed beforehand, making those costs speculative if you are outbid on the day. If you do not have the time to search through a large number of unsuitable properties and have a particular location in mind, house-search companies can be a useful way to find your dream home. Research the company carefully and check that you are paying for architectural

Southsea, Hampshire There are many unlisted Victorian houses in the country where owners have preserved their architectural features, like this one built in 1888.

Blandford Forum, Dorset (Grade II) This eighteenth-century house has been empty for some time, despite being on SAVE's register. The local authority is keen to see it returned to residential use.

expertise, not just locating good schools and railway stations.

Searching your chosen area yourself may highlight a place that looks like the perfect house. If the house is occupied, try putting a carefully worded note through the door asking if it may be for sale in the future. If the property is vacant, it may be worth checking out if the owner is about to sell, and be first in the queue. Ask the neighbours or contact the Land Registry to tell you who owns the site; with a bit of detective work, it should be possible to find out if it is available to purchase. Vacant properties may be the subject of probate, and whilst it may seem heartless to pursue such a property, it is likely to be on the market eventually and the relatives may be happier to sell to a sympathetic individual wanting to live in the house than to a developer.

In the past, developers have avoided buying a house that was listed or in a conservation area, but like everyone else they can now see the insatiable interest in period houses and many are prepared to work with conservation officers if the rewards are there. Some developers have the resources to restore and convert large buildings into apartments and, if the conversion is sympathetic to the fabric of the building, this is another way to become a period home owner without the concerns associated with restoring and owning an individual property. Private individuals looking to buy a residence are still the largest proportion of buyers of listed and period houses of a modest size, although there is a growing number of amateur developers in this category.

Southsea, Hampshire (Grade II) The Royal Marine Barracks (1846) has been renovated and converted into residential units, still retaining some period details.

Planning a Restoration Project

Once a house has been identified, if it is clear that major work is needed the early use of a specialist engineer with experience in the type of structure you are buying is important. In addition, discussions with conservation officers at this stage will establish their ideas on the house and its restoration. This sort of early preparation should enable you to avoid too many costly surprises and help to prioritize finances from the start. Unless you are starting with a total wreck, it is advisable to live in a period house for at least six months before undertaking any major internal work. This allows time to produce detailed records of the house, make informed choices about the use of space and prioritize tasks. Researching into the history of your house and into the period in which it was built, or substantially altered, can help to underpin all future decisions. Spending time searching for information and guidance, contacting societies and companies and planning all proposed work is of paramount importance if mistakes are to be avoided. Through societies and the Internet, buyers of unrestored period properties have a vast wealth of knowledge and expertise at their disposal, but it is important to be able to distinguish reliable advice from the available mass. Information on suitable materials and fixtures and fittings is now much more accessible and many societies have leaflets and courses to assist

you. The Society for the Protection of Ancient Buildings has leaflets concerning the repair of many types of building and, if you are undertaking some of the work yourself, courses are available all over the country.

Unless the house you have bought is a significant Grade II* or Grade I building, you are unlikely to be eligible for any financial assistance when undertaking restoration. However, it is always worth checking with your local council on their policy for issuing grants or loans to support restoration work. Before work starts, locate suitable skilled workers, source sympathetic building materials, discuss plans and ideas with relevant professionals and plan the budget and timescale carefully. If you have undertaken a large house and have no personal time to invest, it is worth considering employing a project manager or, depending on your available time and expertise, a contractor to coordinate the project can prove invaluable. Ensure that your experts are suitably qualified and recommended and do not take the word of a tradesman who stands to benefit financially from the work suggested, unless you are sure that the treatment is in the best interests of the house. Chemical damp treatments on a building that actually requires less invasive remedial work, such as mending gutters and lowering the outside soil level, are typical of

Southampton, Hampshire (Grade II) The interiors of these three houses of 1834 are full of period details and are crying out to be returned to housing, having been used for educational purposes for many years.

the unnecessary and inappropriate work suggested by many tradesmen at the end of the twentieth century.

Creating a habitable, dry house by ensuring that the roof, chimneys and gutters are sound, and that the drains and ground around the house are not encouraging damp, is of primary importance. Unfortunately, this often takes up a large chunk of the budget, especially if there are lead valleys to be replaced, reclaimed clay tiles to be found and repointing of brickwork to be undertaken. There is now an understanding of the importance of recording buildings both before any work is undertaken and during the stages of restoration, and this should include photographing significant alterations and parts of the structure that will eventually be covered over.

Current legislation concerning VAT on the restoration of private houses is no different from any home improvement. Due to European directives the government can only reduce VAT on the repair of churches. Private listed houses can only receive a zero rating on work undertaken if it is a major alteration or conversion. In most cases, this is just what the listing process is trying to control and therefore these two parts of the system seem to be at odds with each other. Lastly, a vacant house undergoing restoration is an easy target for thieves, so insure the property from the moment you buy and include all period items. Many older houses are insured for the standard cost of rebuilding; however, the cost of reproducing a period house and more especially a listed house will always be more expensive than a standard property. The house would have to be rebuilt completely to the 'design, quality and style and in the same materials'. Structural materials, as well as fixtures and fittings, would have to be sourced from specialist firms producing good-quality reproductions, or second-hand items bought at reclamation yards. Either way, rebuilding to you and your conservation officers' standards will far exceed expectations. Many period houses would also require the expertise of specialist builders and craftsmen, and therefore the difference in the cost between a standard rebuild and that of a listed building would have to be met by the owner if the insurance valuation was incorrect at the time of the disaster. Do not rely upon a suggested value by an insurance company but seek specialist advice as to the true cost of reinstating your home. Should you be affected by fire or theft, having plans and photographs of the fixtures and fittings in your house, held away from the premises, is a vital part of the process of protecting your property.

Lavant, West Sussex
There are typical Arts and Crafts features on this house, built in 1912, such as diagonal chimneys and the use of casement windows, but it also has some surprising elements, like open sleeping balconies. A house designed by a notable architect and lovingly restored over a number of decades, it has yet to be listed.

Description

The architects Wells Coates and David Pleydell-Bouverie designed the concept house and a two-storey version was shown at the Ideal Home Exhibition in 1934. The design was intended for use by speculative builders as an alternative to the mock-Tudor dwellings so popular in the 1930s. Several versions of this house were planned, from a five-bedroom house to a small weekend cottage and finally around eighteen were built, including a bungalow. The sun-catching shape, reminiscent of a group of Arts and Crafts houses half a century before, required sliding wrap-around windows and was dependent on the right location to maximize light and view. The construction was designed to be of prefabricated steel with external plaster but, in this example as in many others, the builder used conventional brick for the structure and then plastered over to simu-

Location: Hampshire

Date: 1936

Type   International Style 'Art Deco' (Grade II)

late the original idea. In New Malden, a couple of examples stand out in an avenue of stock-broker Tudor, but the location does not really show their true potential. Although only a handful were ever built, some of the design concepts were taken by speculative builders and became features in standard houses of the

SUNSPAN

period, such as the stucco finish and the more innovative wrap-around window system.

Sunspan, positioned on the south facing slope of Portsdown hill overlooking Portsmouth harbour and beyond to the Isle of Wight, is in the ideal setting for this house. There are two contrasting façades, the north side is low and unimpressive and gives no hint of the exciting south-facing seaward side. The sliding metal-framed windows dominate the southern aspect, looking onto the sundeck and towards the sea in the distance, and both the design and orientation ensure that the main rooms are bathed in light for the whole day.

The interior is no less innovative, with plywood folding doors dividing the main living spaces, a move towards the open-plan living advocated by many architects of this style. The sense of space is emphasised by the 180 degree panoramic view through the windows and takes away the need to decorate the walls with pictures. The main staircase winds around the central chimney-stack and is reminiscent of the earliest medieval stairs, the generally fluid interior is emphasized by the curved walls and doors with flush-fitting fireplaces and minimalist architectural details.

History

Geoffrey Owen Light, a solicitor from Portsmouth, bought the land overlooking Portsea Island and had Sunspan built from the Ideal Home Exhibition design. Shortly after the completion of the house additions were made in the form of recreation space, including a billiard room. During the Second World War its proximity to the naval base made the house seem vulnerable and, after a bomb landed in a field close by, the Lights moved out and the house was requisitioned as a tax office. The house was sold as a private residence after the war, when it gained a basement swimming pool.

The south-facing front of Sunspan is symmetrical, only marred by the strange position of an extension on the middle floor. The contemporary planting echoes the shape of the house and contrasts well with the walls.

The sunburst motif found here on one of the gates can be seen in many houses across the country and is a typical of the 1930s. Elements designed at the same time as the house, such as gates, front doors and windows, are important to the unity of the house.

The front door of Sunspan is on the north side and is made of curved painted plywood. It retains its original chrome door handle and letterbox and leaded stained glass depicting the sunburst motif.

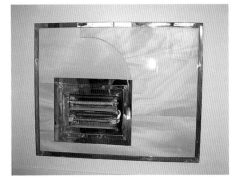

The main fireplace has a fairly standard brick surround, but in other rooms there are metal wall fires with marble-effect backing, as this one from the main bedroom.

Description

Luson is a brick-built villa of Flemish bond under a slate roof with slate hanging to one side, sited on an elevated position on the steep hill above Dartmouth, a town renowned for its buildings of stone and timber. Having been built on this sloping site, the house has three storeys on the seaward side and only two alongside the top road. The south side is symmetrical, with lateral chimney stacks, simple sash windows on the first floor and solidly built stone bays below. The upper part of the bays has a dentil moulding and this may have been echoed along the eaves before a recent alteration to the roof. Stone quoins and rusticated window surrounds with projecting keystones give emphasis to the façade. Although the south-east facing dormer windows are a recent addition, the attic servants' bedrooms (with their own small staircase and windows to the rear)

Location: Devon

Date: 1878

Type: Victorian villa (unlisted)

have been part of the house for some time, and perhaps were originally designed as such. Unusually, the front entrance is at the side of the house, allowing the front rooms to benefit fully from the views and the house is entered through a small porchway with attractive multi-coloured encaustic tiles and half panelling to

LUSON

the walls. The rear of the house, although consisting of mainly service rooms, does sport a multi-pane stained-glass window lighting the stairwell, typical of the late Victorian attention to detail. The architectural details in the interior of the house have remained largely intact and include fireplaces, plasterwork and original kitchen alcove cupboards.

History

Luson was built on a plot of land purchased in 1871 from Sir Henry Seale, the owner of the large mansion called Mount Boone further up the hill. The land was originally kitchen gardens and later allotments leased to local growers and the 1842 Tithe map confirms this. The early patchwork of dividing stone walls still separates parts of the gardens of the new houses along the hill. When the land was sold it included a small brick building which stood close to one of the garden walls and, although it was being used at this time as a dwelling, it clearly had been adapted from an earlier garden house or gazebo (Dartmouth was importing brick for house building as early as 1730). In 1877 James Voisey, a local builder, bought the land and built this handsome double-fronted villa with far-reaching views over the River Dart. This may have been a speculative venture and the house was bought in July 1878 by Henrietta Prideaux, the widow of Samuel Prideaux a local attorney at law. Moving in with her two unmarried daughters and a cook, parlourmaid and housemaid, she named the house 'Luson', meaning in ancient Greek 'future'. The house stayed in the Prideaux family until 1919, when the last daughter Ellen died and son Robert Walter sold the house. Luson has now its fifth owner and it has retained many of its original features and, thankfully, its splendid views of Dartmouth.

The façade is balanced by three windows on the first floor with typical glazing and projecting three-sided bays below, which have an unusual horizontal two-pane arrangement. The original stone walls of the kitchen gardens can be seen here dividing the existing plot into sections.

The fireplace in the main living room is original to the house and the surround is of stone in the solid, simple style of the late Victorian period. The metal insert is very detailed, depicting foliage with Grecian columns at either side, and could probably be found in one of the contemporary pattern books.

The staircase is of the open string type with decorative stair ends and panelling below. The balusters are turned with a hardwood handrail and they end in a circular sweep around the central newel, called a vestigal, in a style popular since the eighteenth century.

Due to this building's position on the hillside, it may have initially been built as a gazebo. There are similarities to octagonal garden buildings seen in a painting circa 1750 of Mount Boone House and its land, in a private collection of the Seale family.

8. ALTERNATIVES TO PERIOD HOUSES

Although owning a period house can be an enriching experience, it is also fraught with practical, financial and ethical issues. Practical considerations revolve around decisions in the maintenance and repair of the fabric of the building and how much one should make use of twenty-first century methods and materials, or whether to be true to the age of the property. In a house that has been developing over a number of centuries this could mean making different decisions for various parts of the house. The knowledge that conservation officers can offer during this process is invaluable, but often relies on both parties being amenable to the role of the other. The decisions reached have financial implications, but more complex are the ethics surrounding the ownership and upkeep of a period house. How much you are house-sitting for future generations, rather than being an owner with the right to alter your environment, is a constant debate, and there will always be a dichotomy between preserving the past and living in the present. Knowledge of the history of domestic architecture ensures that owners are less likely to make decisions in this century which could adversely affect the future of the building or obliterate important historical evidence.

Alternatives to a Period House

Some of the issues concerning period houses and how the owners' decisions affect the future of the house can be avoided by buying part of a larger period building. With the increased shortage of small homes and a downturn in the need for large period buildings, developers are converting the latter into apartments. Owning a slice of history in this way should present fewer concerns and enable a shared enjoyment of a grand property. Alternatively, becoming a tenant

Cerne Abbas, Dorset Although many churches and chapels are listed, it is possible to find later buildings that are not. This conversion is an excellent example of how to do the job sympathetically.

of one of the many smaller National Trust owned houses that are either closed to the general public or only opened occasionally can have all the benefits of period-house living plus the advantage of expert advice on hand.

If you want to exercise greater personal influence over your environment and live in a building that reflects twenty-first-century living

Ottery St Mary, Devon A cob house, in the process of being built in 2002 by Kevin McCabe, is not an imitation of a period house, but is using traditional methods to build a very light and spacious home.

Sedgeford, Norfolk (Grade II) This Civil War powder magazine, circa 1643, was converted into a house in the nineteenth century by adding an upper floor.

requirements, then finding a redundant building to convert into a house may be a more appropriate solution. This has been practised for centuries and past examples across the country include the many monastic buildings altered after the Reformation. Recent examples of exciting conversions, such as redundant water company buildings and a converted London morgue, are properties to which only normal planning regulations apply. Potential grants can be sought to use ecologically friendly products and to develop brown-field sites. Conversions of industrial or commercial buildings, which are less historically significant, can produce interesting

Hayling Island, Hampshire An unusual and comfortable home can be created by converting a sea-going vessel into a houseboat suitable for those who want to downsize to a compact style of living.

homes, although you may find that restrictions could apply to what you may consider to be an architectural wasteland.

New Houses

Often, the attractive qualities of a period house are a solidly built structure, interesting details and a unique design surrounded, in many cases, by other unusual properties. Creating a new house using original methods and materials is another way to acquire these desirable elements and offers an opportunity to express something about living in this age, as much as the Georgian terrace did about the eighteenth century. In the 1930s there was a choice between speculatively built stockbroker Tudor and the steel and glass structures of the International Style, and there is still today a choice between a pastiche of past styles or harnessing traditional building techniques to produce a more contemporary solution. There are a number of companies offering timber-framed houses built from green oak, and there are also some stunning examples where the marrying of traditional methods and avant-garde designs has resulted in innovative and exciting spaces for living. Eco-friendly solutions using early building methods and materials such as cob and straw bale are being explored again by specialist builders and commissioning one of these may create the next generation of period house.

Lodsworth, West Sussex *Using sustainable timber and straw-bale walls, this new cruck-framed house may look a little American Midwest from the outside, but internally the use of windows creates a sense of light and space not known in the cruck houses of the past. (© Ben Law)*

Description

On a steeply sloping site, this house appears to have four entirely different façades with a typical Lutyens mix of the medieval and classical. It is built of standard red brick in Flemish bond under a red tile roof and has four storeys on the lower side and two on the upper part of the hill. However, the view from the road gives no clue as to the unusual nature of the house, where a neo-Georgian entrance leads into the first-floor hall. Other Tudor and Georgian influences can be found both inside and outside, such as rubbed brick mullioned windows on the

Location: Surrey

Date: 1897–99

Type: Arts and Crafts (Grade II*)

The rear elevation is seen here from the bottom of the garden and the full four storeys rise up with the feel of a Tudor gatehouse. Its full-height bays and rubbed brick arches show similarities to New Place in Hampshire, which was built less than a decade later.

THE RED HOUSE

basement level, corner chimneys and keystones on the fireplaces. Inside, the main top-lit staircase (there are also servants' stairs) is pivotal to the design of the interior. It is an open well with closed string treads, which were common in the seventeenth century, and the very central position of the stairwell confirms this early influence. There are three main floors and the basement, but each floor has two levels, giving rise to a confusion of window heights on the four façades. The wrap-around leaded windows on the lower four-storey side offer views across the valley. Although there is a small amount of tiled detailing above one window (a Lutyens trademark), on the whole this house does not have the expensive detailing of other Lutyens' houses. There are no small 'Tudor' bricks as used on other buildings, and the complexities of plan and elevation are produced more by the demands of the site rather than perhaps by the client. Lutyens, although visually influenced by the past, was open to new methods of construction. While other Arts and Crafts architects were studying traditional methods of building, Lutyens was using concrete and steel joists to hold up the floors of the Red House.

History

Edwin Lutyens designed the Red House for the Rev. Henry James Evans, a Charterhouse schoolmaster, who came to Godalming when the school moved from London in 1872. Many masters chose to build houses on this hill, as it is within a short walk of the school and allowed continued links upon retirement. On completion, the house was nicknamed the 'jam factory' by members of the school, presumably as a result of the startling red brick exterior. Evans lived with his wife, daughter and three servants at the Red House from 1899 until his death in 1921. It is easy to see how the strict housemaster might have reacted adversely to Lutyens disappearing off on honeymoon during the building of the house. There are a number of small details where design and execution are not singing from the same hymn sheet and it is surprising that the Rev. Evans did not insist on these being corrected.

The east elevation is three storeys and is dominated by two large chimney stacks. It is a mixture of Tudor-style castellated bays and corner chimneys and the classically influenced porch, with Roman Tuscan columns under a hipped tiled roof.

The staircase of well design has plain diagonally set balusters contrasting with the large vase-shaped finials on square newels. The banister rail and finials were painted at a later stage with flowers and foliage.

On the ground floor, the Butler's pantry still houses an original dresser designed by Lutyens. As was standard at the time Lutyens designed all the details for his houses, including fireplaces and window furniture.

TIMELINE

Date	Monarch	Styles and Movements
1558–1603	Elizabeth I	Elizabethan
1603–25	James I	Jacobean
1625–49	Charles I	Palladianism
		Artisan Mannerism
1649–60	Commonwealth	The Gothic Revival starts
1660–85	Charles II	
		Baroque
1685–89	James II	
1689–94	William & Mary	
1694–1702	William III	
1702–14	Anne	Queen Anne Style
		The Classical Revival
		Late Baroque (Rococo)
1714–27	George I	Early Georgian
		The Palladian Revival starts
1727–60	George II	The Gothic(k) Revival re-starts
1760–1812	George III	Late Georgian
		The Picturesque Movement
		Chinoiserie
1812–20	George III	Regency
1820–30	George IV	Late Regency
		The Greek Revival
1830–37	William IV	Italianate
1837–1901	Victoria	Victorian
		High Victorian Gothic
		Queen Anne Revival
		Arts and Crafts Movement
		The Domestic Revival
		The Aesthetic Movement
		Art Nouveau (European)
1901–10	Edward VII	Edwardian
1910–36	George V	
1936	Edward VIII	Art Deco or International Style
		The Modern Movement
1937–52	George VI	

Date	Events and Innovations
1571	A brick size was established by The Worshipful Company of Tylers and Bricklayers
1579	Act drawn up to stop owners taking windows with them when they moved house
1580	New buildings banned in the City of London in an attempt to control growth
1589	Planning Act restricting building to areas where employment was available
1601	Poor Law Act made the payment of rates compulsory
	Legislation sometime in Jacobean period prohibited the construction of jettied buildings
1662	The Hearth Tax levied on the number of hearths in a house
1666	The Great Fire of London
1667	City of London Building Act to tackle fire resistance and party-wall construction
1676	Palladio's book on architecture translated into English
1683	The Friendly Society of London established, one of the first insurance companies
1689	The Hearth Tax repealed
1696	A Window Tax levied on all but the poorest homes (replaced by another version in 1747)
1706	Turnpike roads began
1707	City of London Building Act to prevent the use of combustible materials on façades
1709	City of London Building Act required windows to be set back 4 inches from façade
1712	A Wallpaper Tax introduced (abolished 1836 for British papers)
1721	The Naval Stores Act lifts the import duty on mahogany
1726	The first architectural pattern book is published
1751	Turnpike Act introduced to organize the upkeep and improvement of roads
1761	The first canal was completed, and named the Bridgewater Canal
1772	Building Act tackling fire resistance and fire prevention
1773	General Turnpike Act amended past private legislation
1774	London Building Act specified sizes of houses into 'rates'
1784	Brick Tax introduced and increased in 1794 and 1803
1797	Window Tax trebled to pay for the war with France
1801	The first population census was taken in England and Wales
1801	First General Enclosure Act introduced in an attempt to standardize various past Acts
1823	A Railway Bill passed to allow trains to carry passengers
1830	Liverpool and Manchester Railway opened
1833	Brick Tax repealed for tiles
1835	Highways Act initiated work on the highways financed by the rates
1848	Public Health Act created Boards of Health to produce local legislation
1850	Brick Tax finally repealed
1851	Window Tax repealed
1851	The Crystal Palace Exhibition Hall built
1866	Labouring Classes Dwelling Act initiated government loans for the building of workers' houses
1868	Artisans Dwelling Act (Torrens Act) gave authorities the power to insist on landlords improving houses
1875	Public Health Act initiated improvements to WCs, sewers and water supplies
1875	Artisans Dwelling Act (Cross Act) began the compulsory purchase of slums
1877	William Morris founded The Society for the Protection of Ancient Buildings (SPAB)
1881	The first garden suburb built in Bedford Park, London
1889	Housing of the Working Classes Act begun the practice of council houses being funded from the rates
1894	Building Act relaxed the rule about recessed windows
1918	Election campaign slogan 'Housing fit for heroes' – David Lloyd George
1919	Addison Act initiated publicly funded housing
1944	The Town and Country Planning Act survey produced the first group of 'listed buildings'

GLOSSARY

Architrave A moulding of wood or plaster originating from the classical orders.

Baluster A vertical support for a handrail that can be turned on a lathe, or cut from a piece of wood and termed a splat or stick baluster. A row of balusters with handrail and newels make up a balustrade.

Bay The divisions of a building defined by vertical elements such as structural timbers, or visually by the position of windows.

Brattishing Ornamental cresting on the ridge of a roof or other surface.

Broken white White paint mixed with a small amount of another pigment.

Burgage Plot A defined area of land chargeable by rent to the crown or local lord of the manor.

Buttress A projection from a wall to strengthen and support.

Canted Cutting off the angle of a square, often found on bay windows.

Carthusian An order of monks.

Caryatid A sculptured female figure used as a supporting column in classical architecture.

Castellated A wall which has defensive indentations called crenellations along its top.

Catslide A long roof, usually at the rear of a building, which often covers an outshut.

Chamfer (bevel) A 45-degree angled cut found along the length of a timber or stone.

Chinoiserie Decorative work popular in the middle of the eighteenth century, inspired by Chinese art.

Claire Voie (or Voyée) A gap or hole in a wall affording far-reaching views, sometimes with inserts of metalwork like grilles.

Classical Pertaining to the architecture of ancient Greece and Rome.

Classical Orders The Greek and Roman system for the arrangement and detailing on column, capital and entablature. The three main types are Doric, Ionic and Corinthian.

Closed-string (staircases) When the stair treads are fixed into the frame and are hidden by a diagonal timber. Open-string stairs have the treads and risers showing.

Column A free-standing upright pillar; an 'engaged' column is attached to the wall.

Colonnade A row of columns.

Conservation Preserving what is there from alteration or destruction.

Corinthian *See* classical orders.

Cottage Ornée A product of the late eighteenth-century picturesque style; a building emulating an English cottage, usually with thatched roof and rustic-style veranda.

Cresting *See* brattishing.

Crow-stepped Referring to the coping, usually on a gable end, originating from the Netherlands.

Dentil Of classical origin, the use of a projecting-block pattern on internal and external decoration in plaster, wood, stone or brick.

Doric *See* classical orders.

Dripstone (hoodmould) A projecting moulding above a door or window to direct water.

Emparking The eighteenth-century practice of moving buildings and whole villages in order to create a landscaped park around a country house.

Fenestration The arrangement of windows on a building.

Gothic Period in architecture from the twelfth to the sixteenth century, epitomized by pointed arches, and whose characteristics were revived in the seventeenth and eighteenth centuries.

Indenture A sealed agreement or contract.

Ionic *See* classical orders.

Keystone The central wedge-shaped stone at the

top of an arch, put in last and often decorated.

Laths Thin strips of wood, woven to form the basis for plaster, also called wattle.

Medieval A period in history usually dated between 1066 and 1485, or up to the dissolution of the monasteries in 1537.
Messuage A dwelling house with outbuildings and land.
Modillion On classical architecture, an ornamental bracket to support a cornice.

Nogging, Brick The use of brick as an infill between timbers on a building.

Obelisk A monumental tapering stone of Egyptian origin.
Ogee A double or 'S' curve: an arch requires two to meet at a point.
Open-String Staircases *See* closed string.
Outshut An extension to the main structure of a building, usually at the rear.

Palladian A symmetrical style of architecture from the ideas of Palladio (sixteenth-century Italian architect) made popular in England in the eighteenth century by Lord Burlington and William Kent.
Papier-mâché A paper pulp used to mould objects and interior architectural decoration.
Parapet A wall extending above the roof height, usually as part of the façade.
Pendant A hanging ornament of wood or plaster used on ceilings, staircases and exposed roof timbers, popular in Jacobean and gothic architecture.
Pentice A small, lean-to roof usually found over a window or door.
Pilaster A shallow rectangular column projecting from a wall.
Plank and Ledge A door made from vertical planks and strengthened behind with horizontal ledges. Described as a ledge-and-brace when diagonal pieces are also added.
Polite Architecture The refined and elegant architecture of the upper classes.

Portico An open porch enclosed by columns that support the roof and usually a pediment.

Quatrefoil Four leaf-shaped curves within a circle or square.

Restoration The act of bringing back an object or building to its original state by a process of repair and replacement. Also the term used for an architectural period between 1660 and 1707.
Rococo A style in the baroque tradition of early eighteenth-century Europe.

Strapwork Interlaced bands of pattern popular in the Elizabethan and Jacobean periods and originating from France and the Netherlands.
Stringcourse A decorative horizontal band of projecting masonry or brick, usually at first-floor level.

Tie Plates Metal plates attached to rods that are fixed through the façade of a building to tie the wall to the structure behind. Often they are evidence of repair work.
Tithe An early tax of one tenth of annual income collected for the church.
Tracery Fine ribwork associated with medieval church architecture and also describing the patterns on fanlights.
Trompe l'Oeil A painting giving the illusion of reality (translation: 'deceives the eye').
Tudorbethan (tudoresque) An early twentieth-century building style using motifs from both Tudor and Elizabethan architecture.
Tympanum A semicircular or pointed panel above a door or window.

Vernacular Architecture Building in an indigenous style with locally found materials, by a craftsman rather than an architect, and built to suit a purpose rather than a fashion.
Vista A controlled, distant view, sometimes framed by trees.

Wainscotting Another word for wall panelling.
Wattle *See* laths.

MUSEUMS, HOUSES AND GARDENS TO VISIT

Reference

The Civic Trust Heritage Open Days –
www.heritageopendays.org.uk
English Heritage – www.english-heritage.org.uk
Historic Houses Association – www.hha.org.uk
Hudson's Guide to Historic Houses and Gardens
– www.hudsons.co.uk
The National Trust – www.nationaltrust.org.uk
Pevsner Guides on-line –
www.lookingatbuildings.org.uk
Welsh Historic Monuments (CADW) –
www.cadw.wales.gov.uk

House History

The National Archives (PRO) –
www.nationalarchives.gov.uk
The National Monuments Record (searchable
public archives) –
www.english-heritage.org.uk

Methods and Materials

Avoncroft Museum of Historic Buildings –
www.avoncroft.org.uk
Beamish Industrial Museum –
www.beamish.org.uk
The Black Country Living Museum –
www.bclm.co.uk
The Weald and Downland Open Air Museum –
www.wealddown.co.uk

House Design and Architectural Details

Brighton Pavilion – www.royalpavilion.org.uk
The Brooking Collection (architectural details),
University of Greenwich – www.gre.ac.uk
The Building of Bath Museum –
www.bath-preservation-trust.org.uk

English Heritage Architectural Study Collection
– www.english-heritage.org.uk
The Geffrye Museum –
www.geffrye-museum.org.uk
The National Art Library (searchable database
of trade catalogues) – www.nal.vam.ac.uk
Museum of Domestic Design and Architecture –
www.moda.mdx.ac.uk
Olga Hirsch Collection at the British Library
(wallpaper) – www.bl.uk
Sir John Soane's Museum – www.soane.org
Temple Newsam House (wallpaper collection) –
www.leeds.gov.uk/templenewsam
Victoria and Albert Museum (collection of interior details) – www.vam.ac.uk
Whitworth Art Gallery (wallpaper and textiles)
– www.whitworth.man.ac.uk

Garden History

The Museum of Garden History –
www.museumgardenhistory.org

A Selection of Houses Open to the Public

(* gardens also worth visiting)

Bedfordshire
Cecil Higgins Art Gallery –
www.cecilhigginsartgallery.org

Cheshire
Little Moreton Hall* –
www.nationaltrust.org.uk

Cumbria
Blackwell – www.lakelandartstrust.org.uk

Derbyshire
Eyam Hall* – www.eyamhall.co.uk
Pickfords House* –
    www.derby.gov.uk/services/museums

Dorset
Fiddleford Manor –
    www.english-heritage.org.uk

East Sussex
Batemans* – www.nationaltrust.org.uk
Charleston* – www.charleston.org.uk
St Mary's House and Gardens* –
    www.yeoldesussexpages.co.uk
The Regency Town House –
    www.regency-town-house.org.uk

Essex
Paycockes – www.nationaltrust.org.uk

Gloucestershire
Chavenage – www.chavenage.com
Holst Birthplace Museum –
    www.holstmuseum.org.uk
Kelmscott Manor – www.kelmscottmanor.co.uk
Owlpen Manor* – www.owlpen.com
Rodmarton Manor* –
    www.rodmarton-manor.co.uk

Hampshire
Jane Austen's House –
    www.janeausten.demon.co.uk

Lancashire
Rufford Old Hall – www.nationaltrust.org.uk

Leicestershire
Newarke Houses Museum –
    www.leicestermuseum.ac.uk

London
Carlyle's House – www.nationaltrust.org.uk
18 Folgate Street –
    www.dennissevershouse.co.uk
Linley Sambourne House – www.rbkc.gov.uk
Handel House Museum – www.handelhouse.org

Merseyside
Speke Hall – www.spekehall.org.uk

Somerset
The Georgian House – www.bristol-city.gov.uk

Suffolk
Gainsboroughs House* –
    www.gainsborough.org
Otley Hall – www.otleyhall.co.uk
South Elmham Hall – www.southelmham.co.uk

Tyne and Wear
Bessie Surtee's House –
    www.english-heritage.org.uk

West Midlands
Selly Manor – www.bvt.org.uk/sellymanor
Soho House – www.bmag.org.uk
Wightwick Manor* – www.nationaltrust.org.uk

West Sussex
The Priest House* – www.sussexpast.co.uk
The Weald and Downland Open Air Museum –
    www.wealddown.co.uk

Wiltshire
The Merchants House –
    www.themerchantshouse.co.uk
Mompesson House* –
    www.nationaltrust.org.uk

Yorkshire
Fairfax House – www.fairfaxhouse.co.uk

Staying in a Period Building

The Landmark Trust –
    www.landmarktrust.co.uk
The National Trust Holiday Cottages –
    www.nationaltrust.org.uk
The Vivat Trust – www.vivat.org.uk
YHA Youth hostels (includes some historic
    buildings) – www.yha.org.uk

A Selection of Gardens Open

(* house also worth visiting)

Bedfordshire
Stockwood Period Gardens –
    www.gardenvisit.com

Buckinghamshire
Chenies Manor House* – www.gardenvisit.com

Cornwall
The Lost Gardens of Heligan –
    www.heligan.com

Cumbria
Levens Hall – www.levenhall.co.uk

Derbyshire
Derby Arboretum – www.derbyarboretum.co.uk
Haddon Hall* – www.haddonhall.co.uk
Melbourne Hall – www.melbournehall.com

Devon
Castle Drogo* – www.nationaltrust.org.uk

Dorset
Kingston Maurward Gardens – www.kmc.ac.uk
Sandford Orcas Manor House* –
    www.gardenvisit.com

East Sussex
Nymans – www.nationaltrust.org.uk
Great Dixter* – www.greatdixter.co.uk

Gloucestershire
Painswick Rococo Gardens –
    www.rococogarden.co.uk
Hidcote Manor Garden –
    www.nationaltrust.org.uk/hidcote

Kent
Sissinghurst Castle Garden –
    www.nationaltrust.org.uk
Groombridge Place Gardens –
    www.groombridge.co.uk

Leicestershire
Belgrave Hall and Gardens –
    www.leicestermuseums.ac.uk

London
Chelsea Physic Garden –
    www.chelseaphysicgarden.co.uk

Somerset
Forde Abbey and Gardens –
    www.fordeabbey.co.uk
Montecute House* – www.nationaltrust.org.uk
No. 4 The Circus –
    www.bath-preservation-trust.org.uk
Barrington Court* – www.nationaltrust.org.uk
Hestercombe Gardens –
    www.hestercombegardens.com

Suffolk
Helmingham Hall Gardens –
    www.helmingham.com

Wales
Aberglasney Gardens – www.aberglasney.org.uk

West Sussex
West Dean Gardens – www.westdean.org.uk

Yorkshire
York Gate Garden – www.perennial.co.uk

USEFUL CONTACTS

Understanding a Period House, its Details and Environment
Association of Genealogists and Researchers in
    Archives – www.agra.org.uk
Cottage Garden Society – www.thecgs.org.uk
Garden History Society –
    www.gardenhistorysociety.org
The Georgian Group –
    www.georgiangroup.org.uk
The Historic Gardens Foundation –
    www.historicgardens.freeserve.co.uk
Images of England (searchable website of listed
    buildings) – www.imagesofengland.org.uk
The National Council for the Conservation of
    Plants and Gardens – www.nccpg.org.uk
Royal Institute of British Architects (RIBA)
    Library and Drawings Collection –
    www.architecture.com
The Society of Architectural Historians of Great
    Britain – www.sahgb.org.uk
The Society for the Protection of Ancient
    Buildings (SPAB) – www.spab.org.uk
Twentieth Century Society –
    www.c20society.org.uk
Vernacular Architecture Group –
    www.vag.org.uk
The Victorian Society –
    www.victorian-society.org.uk
The Wallpaper History Society (details from The
    Victoria and Albert Museum) –
    www.vam.ac.uk

Buying and Legislation
Ancient Monuments Society –
    www.ancientmonumentsociety.org.uk
Architectural Heritage Fund –
    www.ahfund.org.uk
Building Conservation Directory –
    www.buildingconservation.com
'Buildings at Risk' registers can be found at local
    council offices, SAVE Britain's Heritage,
    SPAB, Ancient Monuments Society.
Civic Trust (fosters improvements to the urban
    environment) – www.civictrust.org.uk

Country Life magazine on line –
    www.countrylife.co.uk
Crafts Council (reference library and national
    register of makers) – www.craftscouncil.org.uk
The HM Land Registry – www.landreg.gov.uk
    or – www.landregistrydirect.gov.uk
Listed House Owners Society Club –
    www.listedpropertyownersclub.co.uk
Pavilions of Splendour (period houses for sale) –
    www.heritage.co.uk
The UK Association of Preservation Trusts
    (APT) (full list of all Trusts) –
    www.heritage.co.uk
Website listing property auctions –
    www.propertyauctions.com
Website featuring period houses –
    www.periodproperty.co.uk

Conservation and Courses
The Building Conservation Directory (course
    directory) – www.buildingconservation.com
The Conference on Training in Architectural
    Conservation (COTAC) (list of short courses
    in conservation and crafts) – www.cotac.org.uk
The Conservation Register –
    www.conservationregister.com
The Federation of Master Builders (list of mem-
    bers) – www.fmb.org.uk
The Guild of Master Craftsmen (list of mem-
    bers) – www.thegmcgroup.com
The Heritage Information Trust (register of
    expertise) – www.heritageinformation.org.uk
National Council for Conservation-Restoration
    (conservation groups listed) – www.nccr.org.uk
Princes Foundation (scholarships and training) –
    www.princes-foundation.org
Royal Institute of Chartered Surveyors (list of
    members) – www.ricsfirms.com
Society for the Protection of Ancient Buildings
    (SPAB) – www.spab.org.uk
The Weald and Downland Open Air Museum
    (short courses) – www.wealddown.co.uk
West Dean College (short courses in conserva-
    tion) – www.westdean.org.uk

FURTHER READING

General

The Building Conservation Directory – www.buildingconservation.com

English Heritage (free conservation guides) – www.english-heritage.org.uk

The Georgian Group (publications) – www.georgiangroup.org.uk

The Victorian Society (publications) – www.victorian-society.org.uk

SAVE Britain's Heritage (catalogue of Buildings at Risk) – www.savebritainsheritage.org

The Society for the Protection of Ancient Buildings (SPAB) (publications) – www.spab.org.uk

Fleming, J., Honour, H. and Pevsner, P., *The Dictionary of Architecture and Landscape Architecture* (Penguin, 1999)

Introduction

Clark, P. and Slack, P., *English Towns in Transition 1500–1700* (Oxford University Press, 1976)

Friar, S., *The Local History Companion* (Sutton Publishing, 2001)

Girouard, M., *The English Town* (Yale, 1990)

Lloyd, D.W., *The Making of English Towns* (Gollancz, 1998)

Pevsner, N., *Buildings of England Series* (Oxford University Press, 1995)

House History

Barratt, N., *Tracing The History of Your House* (Public Record Office, 2001)

Cunnington, P., *How Old is Your House* (A. & C. Black, 1988)

Saunders, M., *The Historic Home Owner's Companion* (Batsford, 1987)

Smith, J.T. and Yates, E.M., *Dating of English Houses* (The Journal of Field Studies Council, 1991)

Methods and Materials

Brunskill, R.W., *Brick Building in Britain* (Gollancz, 1990)

Brunskill, R.W., *Timber Building in Britain* (Gollancz, 1999)

Cave, L.F., *The Smaller English House* (Robert Hale, 1981)

Clifton-Taylor, A. and Ireson, A.S., *English Stone Building* (Gollancz, 1994)

House Design

Brunskill, R.W., *Houses and Cottages of Britain* (Gollancz, 1997)

Davey, P., *Arts and Crafts Architecture* (Phaidon, 1995)

Muthesius, S., *The English Terraced House* (Yale, 1982)

Parissien, S., *The Georgian Group Book of The Georgian House* (Aurum Press, revised 1997)

Quiney, A., *The Traditional Buildings of England* (Thames and Hudson, 1990)

Reid, R., *The Georgian House and its Details* (Bishopsgate, 1989)

Architectural Details

Alcock, N.W. and Hall L., *Fixtures and Fittings in Dated Houses 1597–1763* (The Council for British Archaeology, 1999)

Calloway, S., (ed.) *The Elements of Style* (Reed International Books Ltd, 1996)

Lander, H., *House and Cottage Restoration* (Acanthus Books, 1999)

Miller, J. and M., *Period Details* (Mitchell Beazley, 1987)

Saunders, G., *Wallpaper in Interior Decoration* (V&A Publications, 2002)

Garden History

Longstaffe-Gowan, T., *The London Town Garden 1700–1840* (Yale University Press, 2001)

Strong, R., *The Artists and the Garden* (Yale University Press, 2000)

Strong, R., *The Renaissance Garden in England* (Thames and Hudson, 1998)

Stuart, D., *The Plants that Shaped our Gardens* (F. Lincoln, 2002)

Turner, T., *English Garden Design* (Antique Collectors Club, 1986)

The National Gardens Scheme Guide (The National Gardens Scheme)

Titchfield, Hampshire (Grade II) *The old door at Mayburys.*

INDEX

Numbers in italics refer to illustrations in the text.